# 11+ Non Verbal Reasoning

## The
# Non-Verbal Ninja
## Training Course

## Book 3
# Matrices
# and Groups

CEM-style Practice Exam Paper Questions
with *Visual* Explanations

Eureka! Eleven Plus Exams

## The Eureka! 11+ Confidence series
CEM-style Practice Exam Papers covering:
Comprehension, Verbal Reasoning,
Non-Verbal Reasoning and Numerical Reasoning

## Numerical Reasoning: Advanced Training Workbooks

Tough exam paper questions and detailed explanations of
how to tackle them, to increase speed and reduce error.

## Verbal Reasoning: Advanced Training Workbooks
The *1000-Word Brain Boost* is a powerful, intensive course teaching
Synonyms, Antonyms, Odd-One-Out, Analogy, Vocabulary and Cloze in
CEM-style questions. Its famous *Explanations* section explains
hundreds of language subtleties and distinctions that
many 11+ candidates find challenging.

## Non-Verbal Reasoning: The *Non-Verbal Ninja* Training Course
The *Non-Verbal Ninja* is an intensive *visual* course for core CEM exam skills. The
3 training workbooks include over 600 puzzles coupled with *visual* explanations.
They build both fundamental skills and the crucial confidence to seek out rules
without having to have them explained first. Each book rapidly moves on from
simple levels to challenging training puzzles that enhance the capacities of even
the strongest 11+ hopefuls.

Please check the website **www.eureka11plus.org/updates** for updates and clarifications for this book.

Copyright © Eureka! Eleven Plus Exams 2016
Best-selling, realistic, 11+ exam preparation series

Publication date: 1 January 2016
Revision date: 15 January 2016.
First published in the United Kingdom by  Eureka! Eleven Plus Exams
http://www.eureka11plus.org  ·  Email: office@eureka11plus.org

ISBN-13: 978-1522935209
ISBN-10: 1522935207

We are all human and vulnerable to error. Eureka! Eleven Plus is very grateful to any reader who notifies us on
office@eureka11plus.org of an unnoticed error, so we can immediately correct it and provide a tangible reward.

# Non-Verbal Ninja

Non-verbal reasoning questions in the 11+ exam provoke anxiety amongst students and parents alike, since the test seems, at first, to be unlike the activities of normal everyday life. In reality, however, it is straightforward to train to improve one's performance in these puzzles.

The *Non-Verbal Ninja Training Course* from Eureka! Eleven Plus Exams is a three-part series of training books with several features to maximise the skill boost they provide to students.

- Full explanations are given immediately after each block of questions

- **Visual explanations** are provided where these are easier to understand

- The early questions of each type are easy, testing only one or two rules

- Challenging, broad-ranging questions are soon introduced

- Each question teaches an additional skill or reinforces a core skill

- You are **not** told in advance exactly what the rule will be, so you build confidence in identifying the rule for yourself — a crucial skill for exam success

The series of books, studied in sequence, covers the spectrum of types of format of questions and of the types of rule being tested. Some rules can be tested in many different settings.

Dedicated practice and, more importantly, careful review of the explanations of questions that turned out to be difficult, is the key to success in Non-Verbal Reasoning.

# Become an 11+ Non-Verbal Ninja!
To gain the most from this course, follow the path of success

**Focus on learning as many new rules as possible**
Look forward to finding many questions you cannot answer correctly at first, as these are what make the training worthwhile.

**Expect the first few questions of each type to be easy**
Do not skip ahead if questions seem easy. Each is building up your experience which you may need to draw upon for later questions. The questions quickly become more difficult.

**While training, spend as much time as you need**
The Ninja Training Course is not a race. Savour the learning and be enriched by it. The longer you spend thinking about all possible solutions to a problem, the more you will learn when the explanation is revealed.

**Bite size**
If you are studying in short chunks of time, plan ahead so that you have time to *review the explanations*. For example, if you only have a few minutes, you might tackle one page and carefully read the answers and explanations for it.

**"I give up"?**
Top ninjas don't just give up. They learn from challenging questions by writing a list of rules that they tried, and why they didn't work. Strike out the options that you know to be wrong, and indicate why. This could be diagrammatically, as you see in the answer pages. The more care you put into these baffling questions, the more you will learn from the explanation, and the more easily you will recognise this rule in the only questions that really matter — the ones in the exam.

**Work steadily through the books of the course**
The principles in book 1 are applicable throughout the training course, as they can be tested in many types of question.

**Practice entire papers**
Entire exam papers consist of non-verbal reasoning questions mixed in with other types. Use the *11+ Confidence* family of Practice Exam Papers to build your experience of this variety.

# Training Session 1

There is a 3x3 grid of cells, each containing a design. The design of one cell is hidden. Of the 6 options on the right, which design would be most suitable for the hidden cell?

Circle the letter you choose. As part of your training, write on the options you reject a short note or mark indicating why you are rejecting them. Give yourself as much time as you need to solve the puzzles. After you have done your very best, review the explanations that follow this session.

## Question 1

During your exam you will not be told for each non-verbal reasoning question what rule is being used to transform one cell into the next: you will have to work it out for yourself.

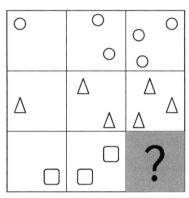

This ninja training course teaches you this experience of discovery, with visual explanations

This is the easiest question in the entire course – enjoy!

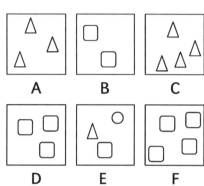

## Question 2

This is only slightly more difficult, testing two principles together.

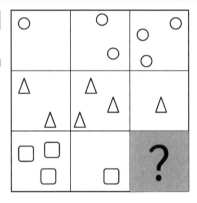

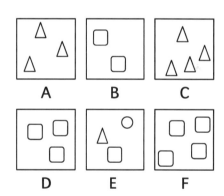

## Question 3

Now use your ninja skills from the above two questions to tackle one with three principles in the same question.

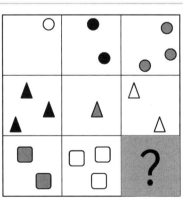

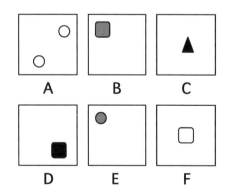

5

Go to the next page ➡

Question **4**

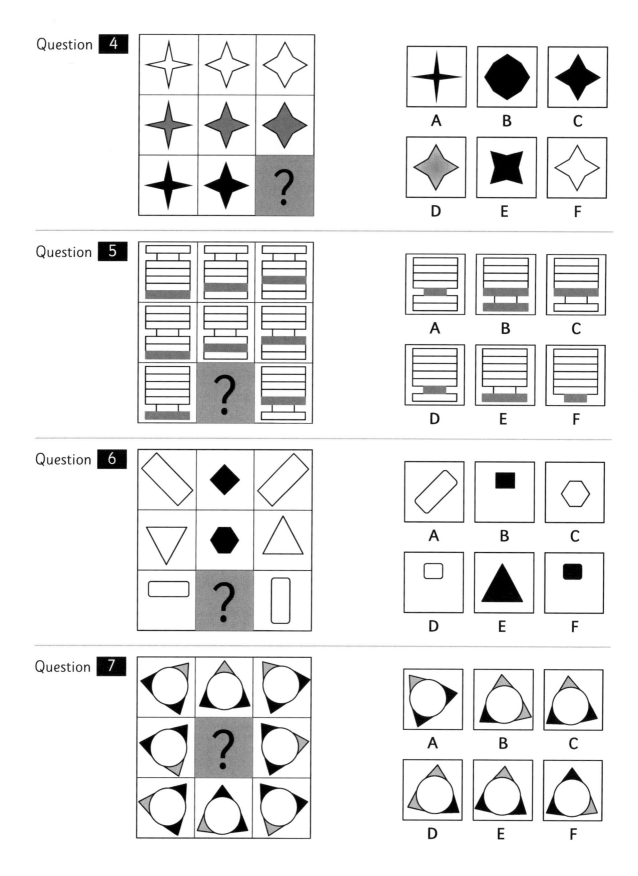

Question **5**

Question **6**

Question **7**

Go to the next page ➡

Question **8**

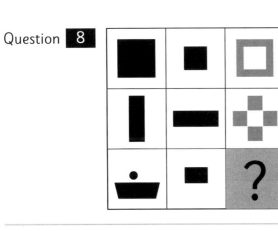

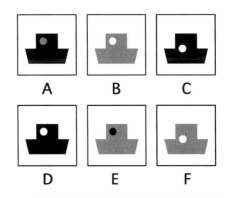

A     B     C

D     E     F

Question **9**

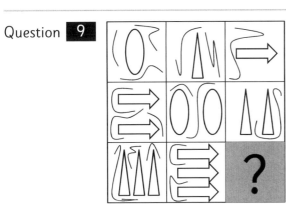

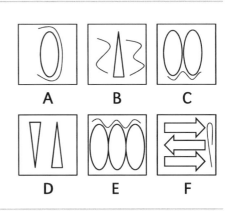

A     B     C

D     E     F

Question **10**

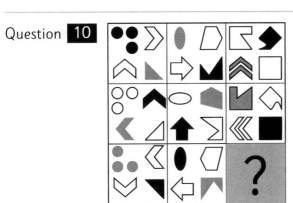

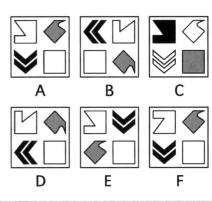

A     B     C

D     E     F

Question **11**

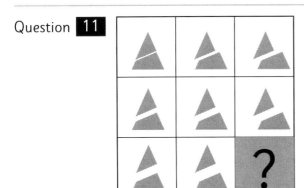

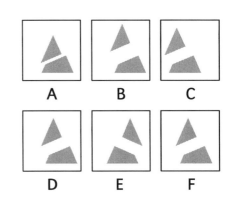

A     B     C

D     E     F

Go to the next page ➡

Question **12**

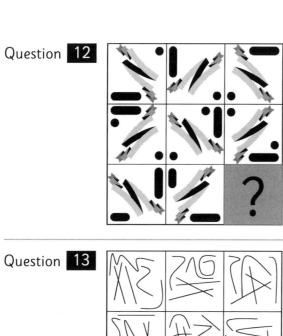

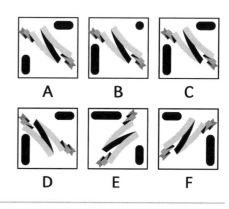

A     B     C

D     E     F

Question **13**

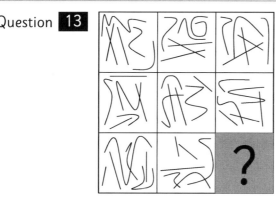

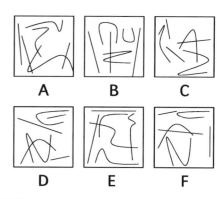

A     B     C

D     E     F

Question **14**

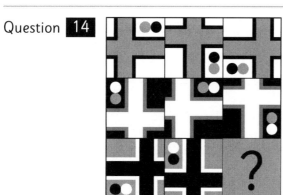

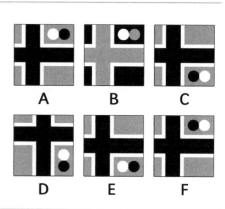

A     B     C

D     E     F

Question **15**

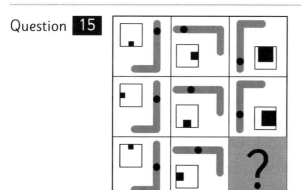

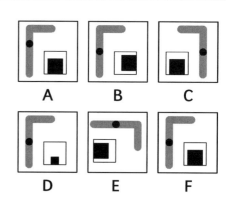

A     B     C

D     E     F

This is the end of this session.

# Answers to Session 1

If you have completed Book 1 of the course, you will have found these questions simple.
To get the most from this course, don't just mark your answers right or wrong. Read the explanations and examine the diagrams which show you how examiners think. Skilled ninjas know how important it is to understand your adversary!

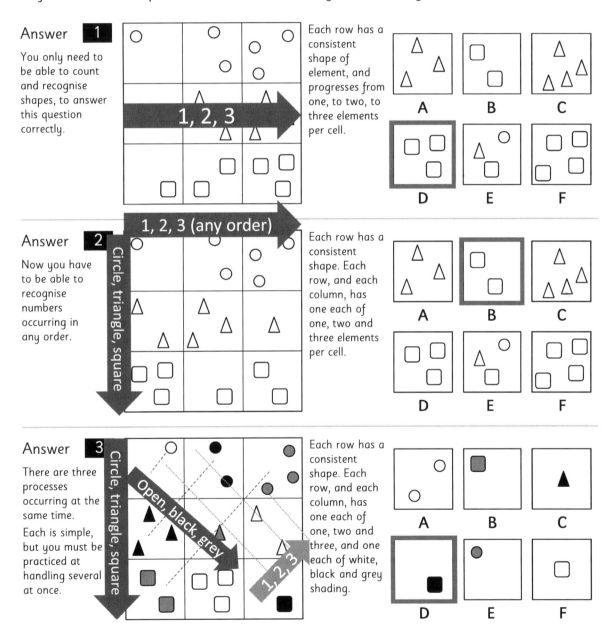

Answer **1**

You only need to be able to count and recognise shapes, to answer this question correctly.

Each row has a consistent shape of element, and progresses from one, to two, to three elements per cell.

Answer **2**

Now you have to be able to recognise numbers occurring in any order.

Each row has a consistent shape. Each row, and each column, has one each of one, two and three elements per cell.

Answer **3**

There are three processes occurring at the same time.

Each is simple, but you must be practiced at handling several at once.

Each row has a consistent shape. Each row, and each column, has one each of one, two and three, and one each of white, black and grey shading.

## Answer  4

In this question you have learned about progressive change in shape.

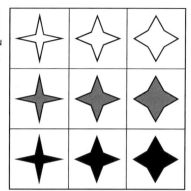

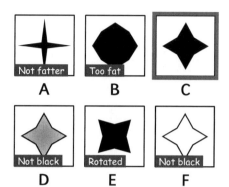

## Answer 5

The narrow rectangles move down two positions from one row to the next.

The grey shading rises by one position from one column to the next.

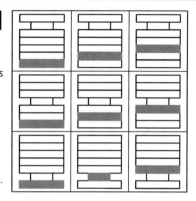

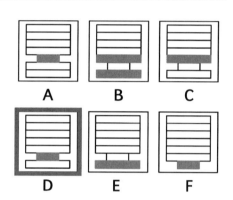

## Answer 6

The central cell in each row contains a shaded version of exactly the overlap region between the elements in the left and right cells in that row.

Notice that the overlap has to be exactly matched, so that (in the case of the unknown cell) its corners are sharp, and not rounded like the left and right elements.

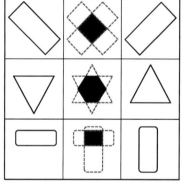

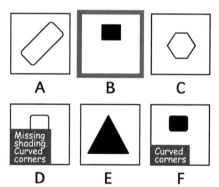

## Answer 7

Within each column, the three prongs retain their orientations, with each prong taking it in turn to be grey.

Within each row, the shape rotates slightly (30 degrees) anticlockwise.

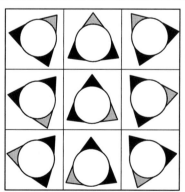

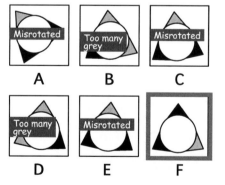

Go to the next page

## Answer 8

In each row, the shapes in the left and middle cells are merged to make the shape in the right cell. Where there is black in *only one* of the left or the middle cell, the right cell is grey.

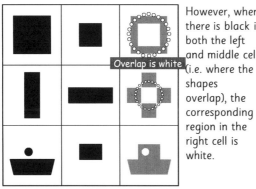

However, where there is black in both the left and middle cell (i.e. where the shapes overlap), the corresponding region in the right cell is white.

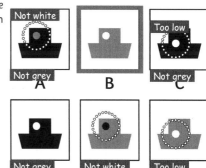

## Answer 9

Each row has one or more big ovals in one cell, one or more big triangles in another cell, and one or more big arrows in another cell.

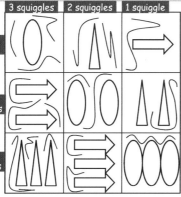

The numbers of big elements and of squiggles also varies with the columns and rows as shown here.

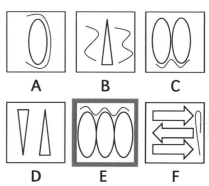

## Answer 10

Each cell has four quarters, each with a shape (which may be made of several elements, e.g. 3 discs). Within each column, from top to bottom, the shapes in each quarter rotate 90°

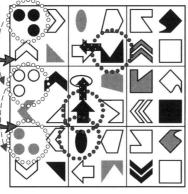

anticlockwise (highlighted in the left column).

Separately, the shading pattern rotates clockwise around the whole cell (highlighted in the middle column).

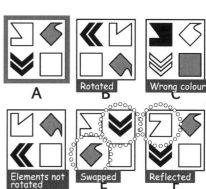

## Answer 11

Moving down from one cell to the one below, the upper triangle moves up (highlighted by the vertical scale).

Moving right from one cell to the next, the lower shape moves one step to the right

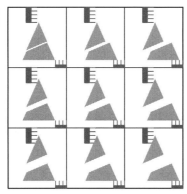

(highlighted by the horizontal scale).

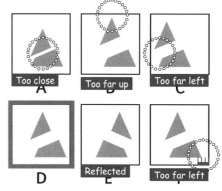

Go to the next page ➡

## Answer  12

In each row, from left to right the cells rotate clockwise.

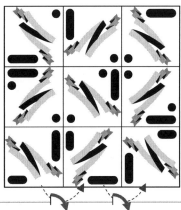

Too small
A

Too small
B

C

Ribbon rotated
D

Rotated
E

Reflected
F

## Answer 13

Each cell has three straight lines and three curved lines. In the top row, all crossings are between two straight lines. In the bottom row, all crossings are between two curved lines.

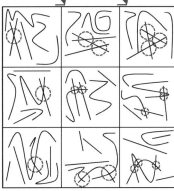

In the middle row, all crossings are between a curved and a straight line. In the left column, there is 1 crossing. In the middle, there are 2. In the right column, there are 3.

Too many crossings

Wrong type of crossings

Wrong type of crossings

D

Too many of the lines are curved

Too few crossings

## Answer 14

Within each row, at each step the design rotates clockwise, and then the two discs exchange places.

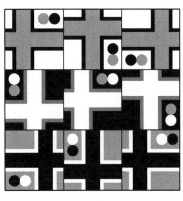

**Tip:** as soon as you see two answers (A and E) that look similar, examine the question carefully for unnoticed rotations or (in this case) reflections or swappings

A

B

Wrong side
C

Rotated
D

Wrong side
E

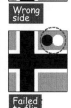
Failed to flip
F

## Answer 15

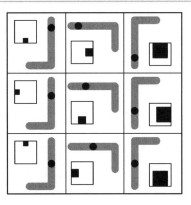

Too far up
A

Rotated
B

Reflected
C

Too small
D

Rotated
E

F

12      This is the end of this session. ✖

# Training Session 2

Well done, young ninja! You have completed training in detecting several types of rule: counting, size, colour and rotation.

This session brings in some new rules. Again, we won't tell you what they are in advance because true ninjas learn to recognise and respond to unplanned situations.

Question **1**

This question brings something new.

Question **2**

Question **3**

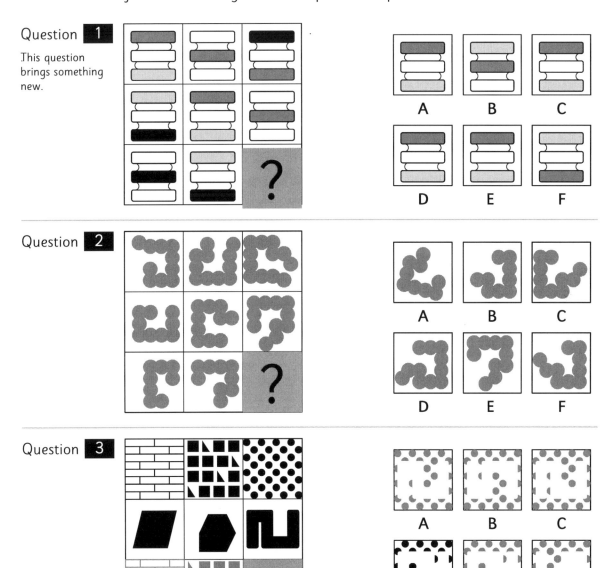

Go to the next page ➡

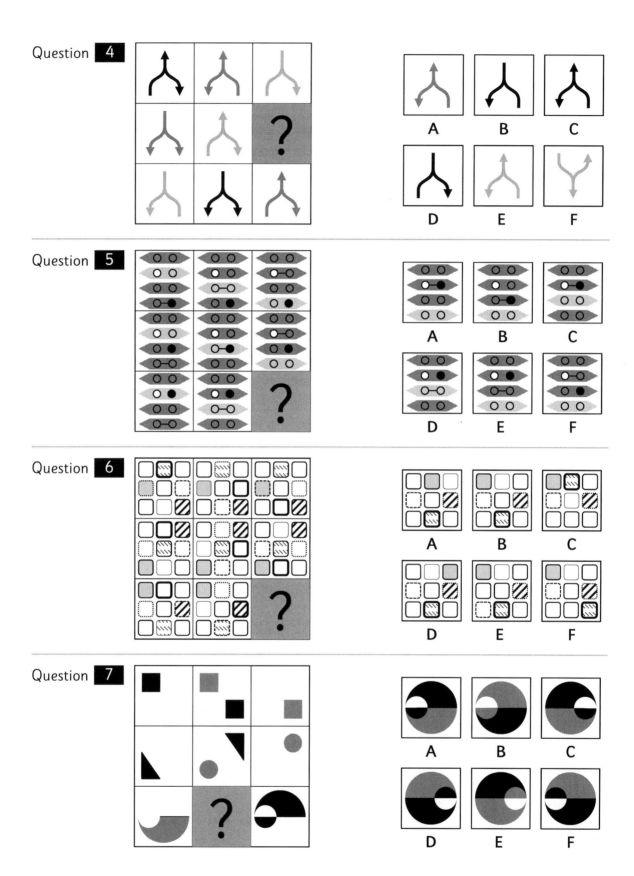

Question **4**

Question **5**

Question **6**

Question **7**

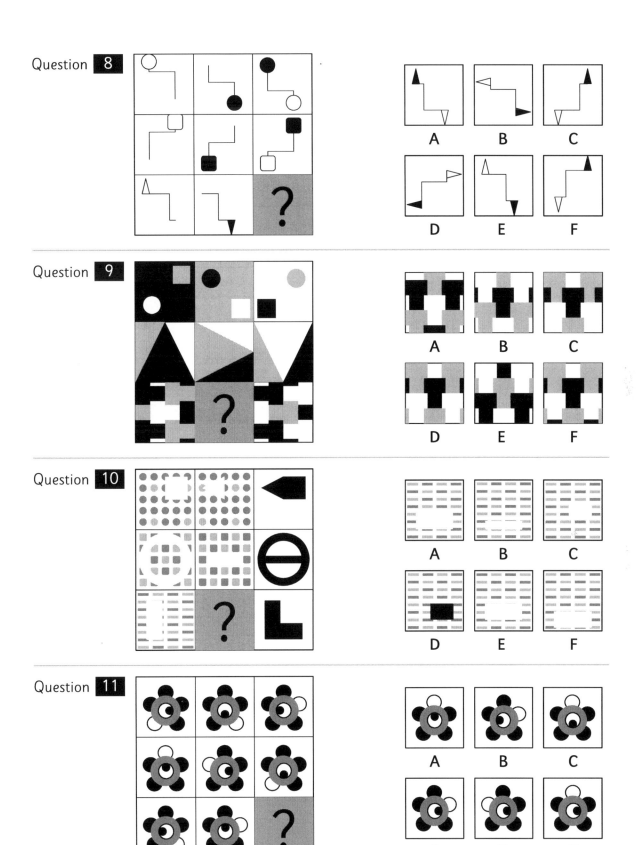

Question 8

Question 9

Question 10

Question 11

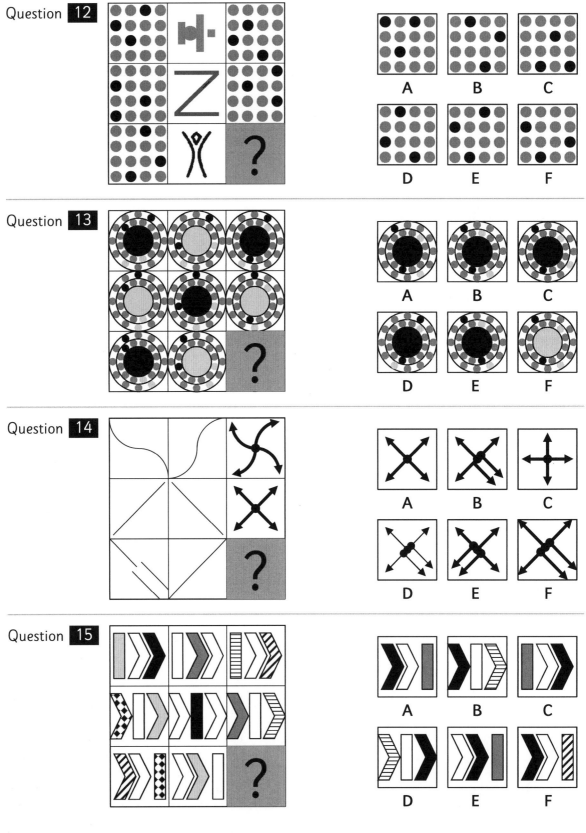

This is the end of this session.

This session has taught you some new rules, as well as revised the simpler rules. More importantly, you have learned to detect the rules without advance warning of what the rules will be in each question: vital training for your forthcoming exam.

## Answer  1

The shading is consistent along the top-left to bottom-right diagonal (as shown by the dashed squares).

The curves on the *left* side are consistent in each row.

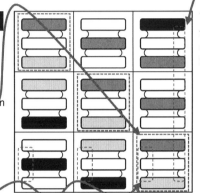

The curves on the *right* side are consistent in each column.

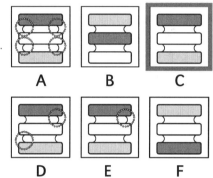

## Answer 2

The design rotates clockwise. In each step down, an element is removed from one end of the chain, as shown by the arrows and dotted circles in the left column.

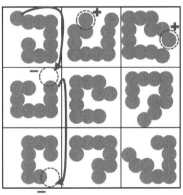

Meanwhile, in each step across, an element is added at the other end of the chain, as shown by the dotted circles in the top row.

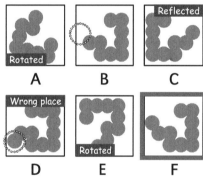

## Answer 3

Notice that the background pattern (from the top row) moves before it appears, in grey, in the bottom row. It is easiest to see in the middle column that the movement is downward (with bottom row moving to top.)

The middle column also confirms that the big central element simply changes from black to white but does not rotate, so the S shape in the final column must stay in the same position.

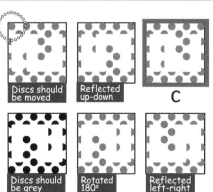

Go to the next page ➡

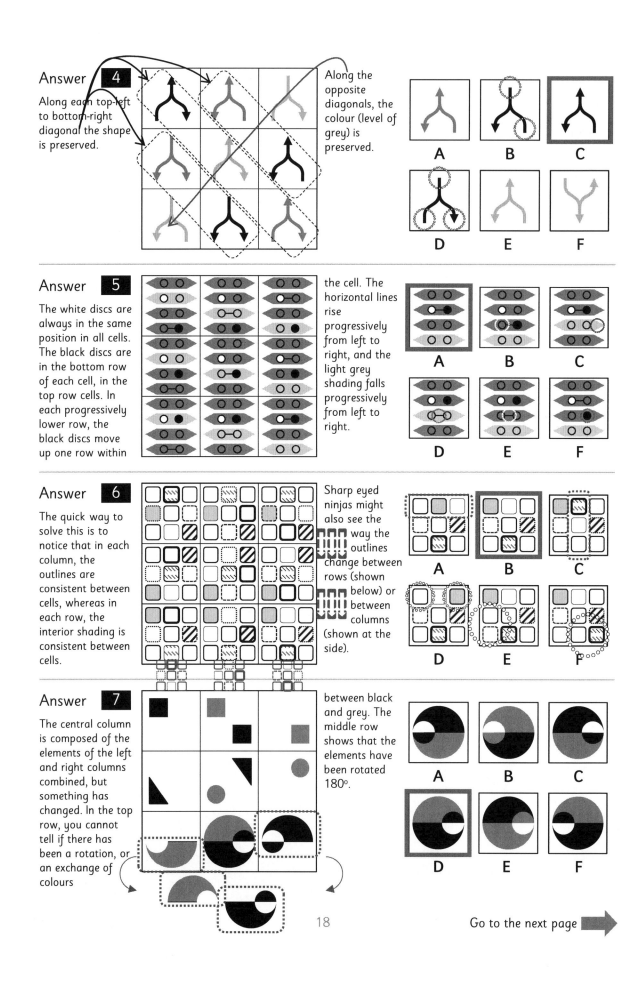

**Answer** 4

Along each top-left to bottom-right diagonal the shape is preserved.

Along the opposite diagonals, the colour (level of grey) is preserved.

**Answer** 5

The white discs are always in the same position in all cells. The black discs are in the bottom row of each cell, in the top row cells. In each progressively lower row, the black discs move up one row within

the cell. The horizontal lines rise progressively from left to right, and the light grey shading falls progressively from left to right.

**Answer** 6

The quick way to solve this is to notice that in each column, the outlines are consistent between cells, whereas in each row, the interior shading is consistent between cells.

Sharp eyed ninjas might also see the way the outlines change between rows (shown below) or between columns (shown at the side).

**Answer** 7

The central column is composed of the elements of the left and right columns combined, but something has changed. In the top row, you cannot tell if there has been a rotation, or an exchange of colours

between black and grey. The middle row shows that the elements have been rotated 180°.

Go to the next page

## Answer 8

The central element is a 3-part line. The middle part moves progressively from the left cell to the right cell, with the other parts changing length as required to keep the start and end points fixed (see arrows).

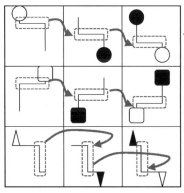

Meanwhile the first column has a white element at the top, the second column a black element at the bottom, and the third column a black element at the top and white element at the bottom.

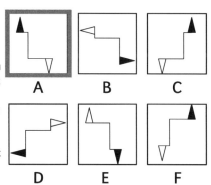

## Answer 9

In each row, from one cell to the cell on the right, the shape rotates clockwise 90°.

Meanwhile the shading also changes (as shown in the figure)

Black becomes grey, grey becomes white, white becomes black.

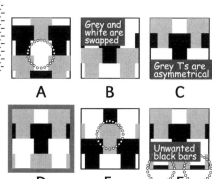

## Answer 10

Between the left column and the middle column, the background grey pattern shifts one element to the left. The dotted circles and the arrows show this in the top row.

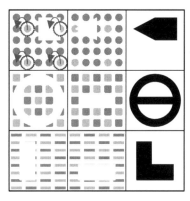

Meanwhile the white foreground elements in the left and middle columns are combined to make a black shape in the right column.

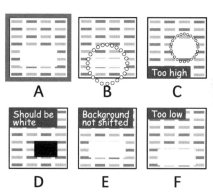

## Answer 11

The inner shape rotates 90 degrees clockwise with every step to the right, and 90 degrees anticlockwise with every step down.

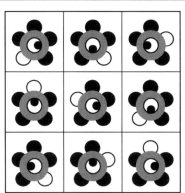

The white disc moves one step anticlockwise with every step to the right, and two steps clockwise with every step down.

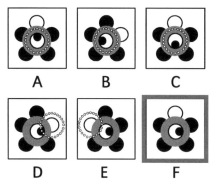

Go to the next page

## Answer 12

In each row, the left cell is reflected or rotated to form the right cell. The middle column indicates what form of symmetry to apply.

In the top row, the middle cell has mirror symmetry

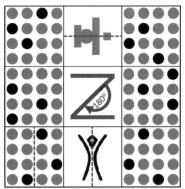

with a horizontal mirror line.

In the second row, it is rotation by 180 degrees.

In the bottom row, it is reflection in a vertical mirror line.

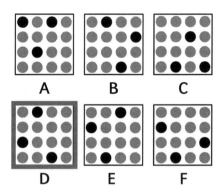

## Answer 13

The outer ring of elements rotates one step anticlockwise with each move down a cell, and the inner ring rotates two steps anticlockwise with each move right a cell.

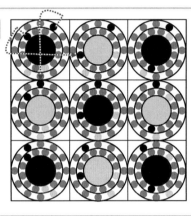

The inner disc alternates in colour between black and grey.

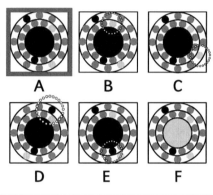

## Answer 14

This is easy if you remember that when objects are rotationally symmetrical, you cannot tell if they have been rotated. The rule is that the shapes in the first and second columns are combined to

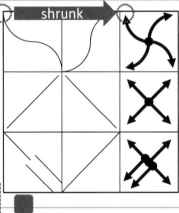

make the third column, with each line replaced by an arrow, each meeting point of lines marked with a black blob, the resulting shape shrunk slightly, and rotated 90° clockwise.

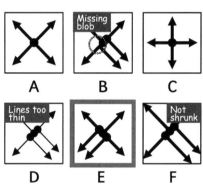

## Answer 15

Within each row the shapes are constant in the 3 cells of the row. From one row to the row below, the shapes move right one position, and the shading moves forward *two* positions.

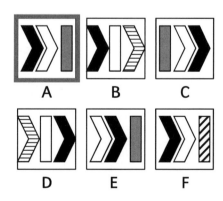

This is the end of this session. ⊗

# Training Session 3

Now you have command of a large number of types of rule. They will come at you thick and fast from now on, with occasional new rules being added.

Keep alert in your practice, young ninja!

Question **1**

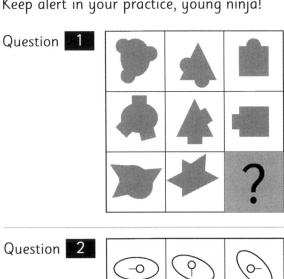

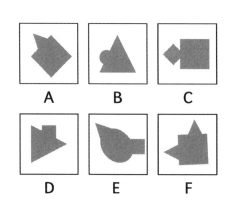

Question **2**

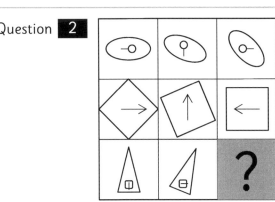

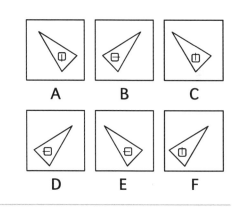

Question **3**

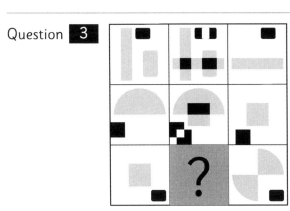

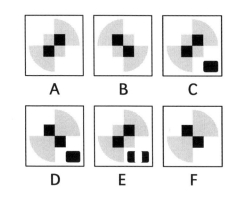

Go to the next page

Question 4

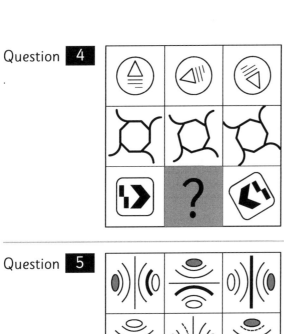

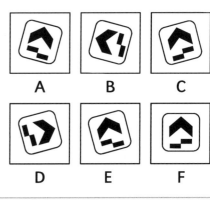

A　　B　　C

D　　E　　F

Question 5

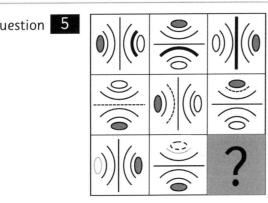

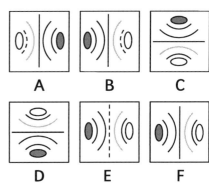

A　　B　　C

D　　E　　F

Question 6

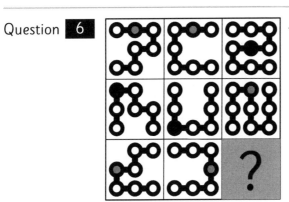

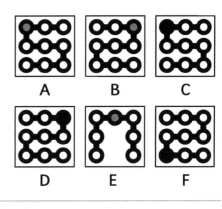

A　　B　　C

D　　E　　F

Question 7

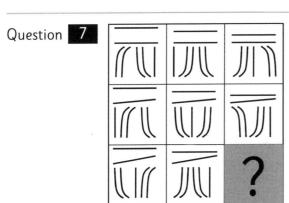

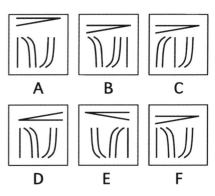

A　　B　　C

D　　E　　F

Go to the next page

Question  8

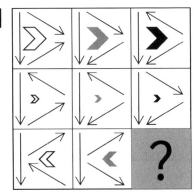

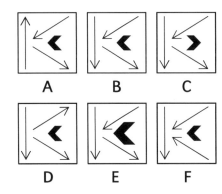

Question 9

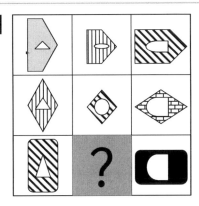

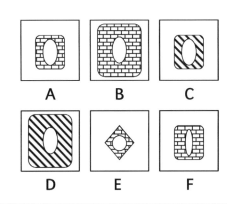

Question 10

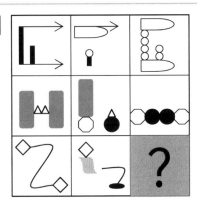

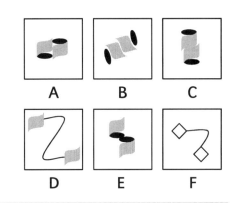

Question 11

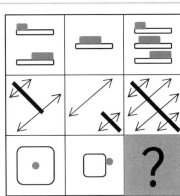

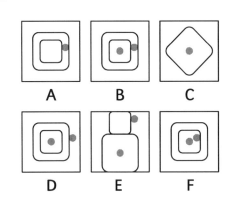

Go to the next page

Question **12**

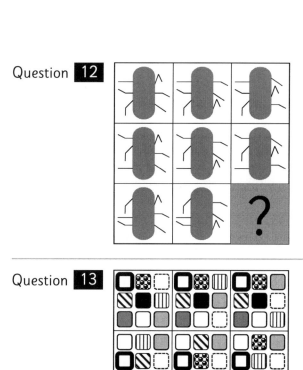

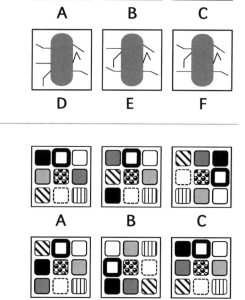

Question **13**

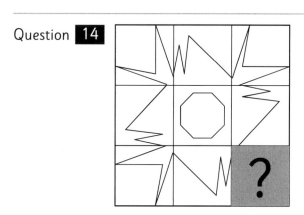

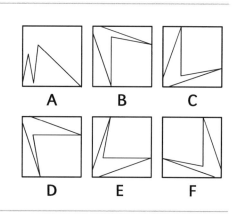

Question **14**

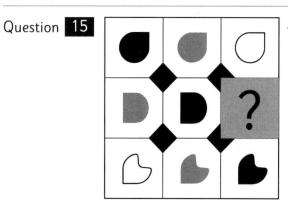

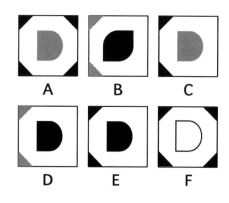

Question **15**

This is the end of this session.

# Answers to Session 3

Combining your skills from Book 1 and the experience from the previous sessions of this book, you now have command of almost all the rules that can apply to matrices.

You are now entering the advanced area of the ninja training course. We will focus not on the simpler end of the exam spectrum (which almost all candidates can do) but the harder end where training matters and separates the high-achieving ninjas from the others.

## Answer 1

Each cell has a large central shape and one or more small elements overlapping it.

In the left column, the central shape is an oval; in the middle, a triangle; in the right, a square.

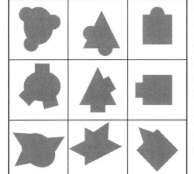

In the top row the small elements are 3, 2 and 1 disc respectively. In the second, they are 3, 2 and 1 squares. In the third, it is 3, 2 and 1 triangles.

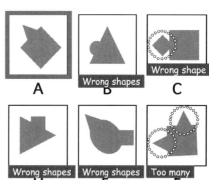

## Answer 2

In each row (highlighted in the top row), the outer shape rotates clockwise one sixteenth of a turn (that is to say, two steps make 45 degrees, which is 1/8 of a turn).

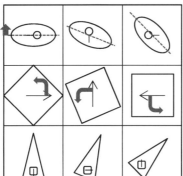

Meanwhile the inner shape rotates anticlockwise 90 degrees (highlighted by the curved arrow in the second row).

## Answer 3

In the middle column, the elements of the left and right cells are drawn overlapped.

Where two black elements overlap, the middle column shows white.

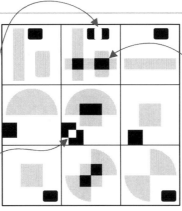

Where two grey elements overlap, the middle column shows black.

Perfect overlap, so black + black gives white (i.e. disappears)

Go to the next page ▶

## Answer 4

The middle row is unhelpful because it has so much rotational symmetry. The top row, on the other hand, tells us that there is an anticlockwise rotation by slightly more than 90°.

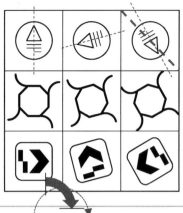

The second rotation produces a total of just over 180°. In fact it is still visibly less than 180+45 (thick dashes). It turns out to be 180+30, with each step being 90+15 degrees.

**A**     **B**     **C**

**D**     **E**     **F**

---

## Answer 5

At each step to the right, the design rotates clockwise. At each step down, the design rotates anticlockwise.

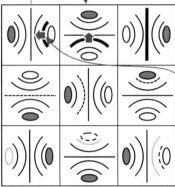

At each step to the right, the pattern of the (thick or dashed or pale-coloured) moves one element closer to the grey shaded element.

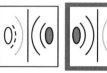  

**A**     **B**     **C**

**D**     **E**     **F**

---

## Answer 6

In each column (one is highlighted as an example), the design rotates anticlockwise. One of the central regions of the rings is shaded (grey or black) and its position moves progressively along

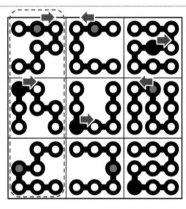

the chain of rings, alternating in colour between grey and black.

**A**     **B**     **C**

**D**     **E**     **F**

---

## Answer 7

The uppermost line is highest in the left column, and descends by one step in each subsequent column.

The second line tilts up to the right progressively with each row, from flat in the top row.

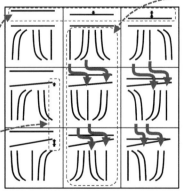

In each column, the three lower symbols (two of which are pairs of elements) move rightwards, with the rightmost one wrapping back to the left

  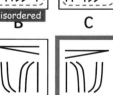

**A**     **B**     **C**

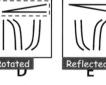

**D**     **E**     **F**

Go to the next page

## Answer 8

In each row, from left to right the move from left to middle cell reverses the lower diagonal arrow, and the move from middle to right cell reverses the upper diagonal arrow.

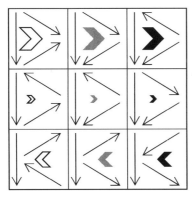

Meanwhile the central chevron becomes darker, from unshaded to grey to black.

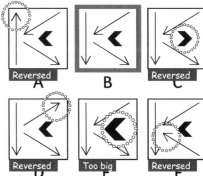

## Answer 9

From left to right, the outer shape first becomes shorter in height (without changing in width) and then becomes wider (without changing in height, see horizontal dashes). From top to

bottom, the inner shape becomes shorter in height, without changing in width (see dotted lines). Shading is consistent in a diagonal direction.

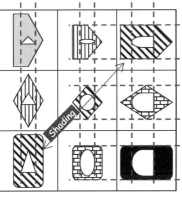

A    B    C

D    E    F

## Answer 10

The middle column indicates what replacements to make to the elements in the left column to make the third column.

The elements from the left cell lie on the outside part of the middle cell, and

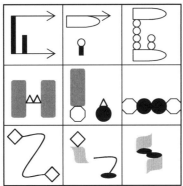

the elements for the right cell lie on the inside part of the middle cell.

D    E    F

## Answer 11

The right cell in each row is composed of the combination of the elements in the left and middle cells.

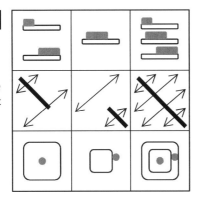

A    B    C

D    E    F

Go to the next page ➡

## Answer 12

The left set of legs of this insect are constant within each row (shown by bold dashes in the top row, as an example).

The right set of legs are constant within each column (shown by the fine

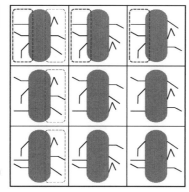

dashes in the left column). The left legs move up between rows; the right legs move down between columns but you don't need to discover this to answer correctly.

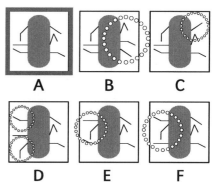

## Answer 13

In each row of the matrix, one column of elements is shuffled upwards as your eye moves right. The top element, when it moves up out of the cell, reappears at the bottom.

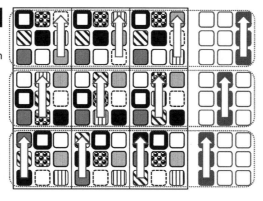

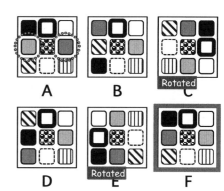

## Answer 14

The outer eight cells contain a continuous line. All four corner cells are identical, apart from being rotated 90° in relation to the neighbouring corner cells.

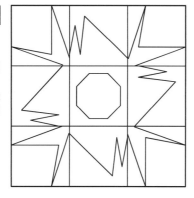

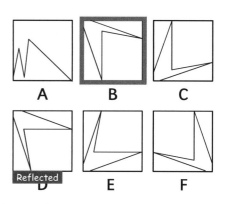

## Answer 15

The central element has the same shape within each row (e.g. D shape in the middle row). Its colour is consistent in each top-left-to-bottom-right diagonal direction. (Do not assume that there must be

one of each colour in a row.)

The entire matrix has black corners where required to give diamonds at all four corners of the central cell.

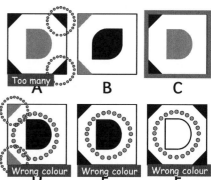

This is the end of this session.

# Training Session 4

In this style of question, you are shown a few members of a group, and a series of options, with your task being to choose which option is most likely to fit into the group.

Armed with your Non-Verbal Ninja training you should be able to compose several possible rules. Quite often the challenge is that you must find a rule which enables the selection of *just one* of the options. We will start with easy questions.

Question **1**

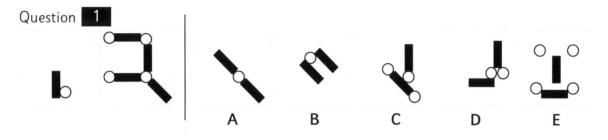

A          B          C          D          E

Question **2**

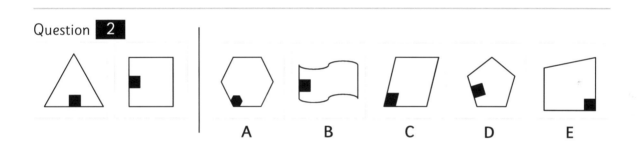

A          B          C          D          E

Question **3**

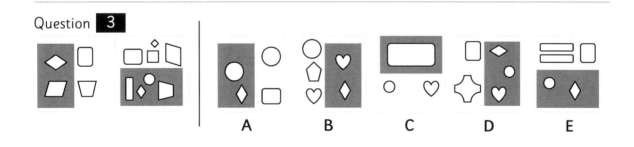

A          B          C          D          E

Go to the next page

## Question 4

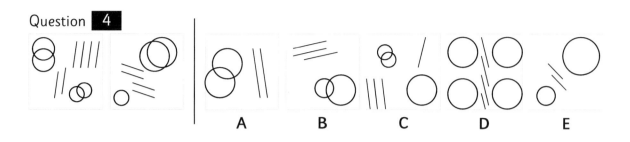

A     B     C     D     E

## Question 5

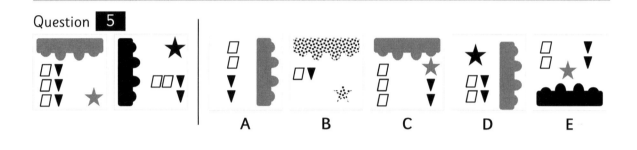

A     B     C     D     E

## Question 6

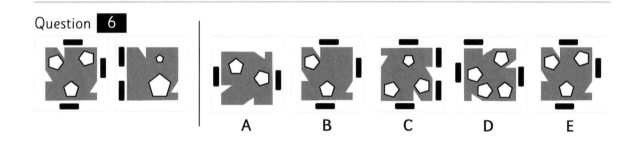

A     B     C     D     E

## Question 7

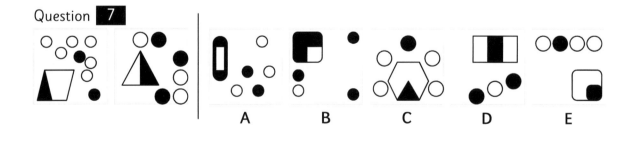

A     B     C     D     E

Go to the next page

Question

  |

A      B      C      D      E

Question 9

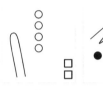    

A      B      C      D      E

Question 10

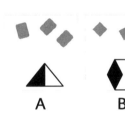   

A      B      C      D      E

Question 11

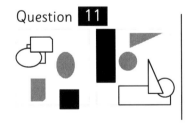 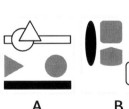 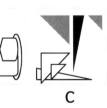  

A      B      C      D      E

Go to the next page

**Question 12**

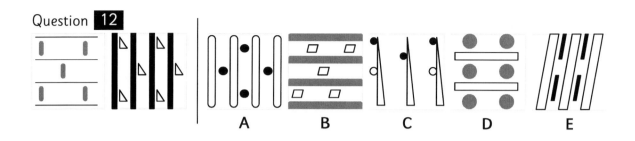

A      B      C      D      E

**Question 13**

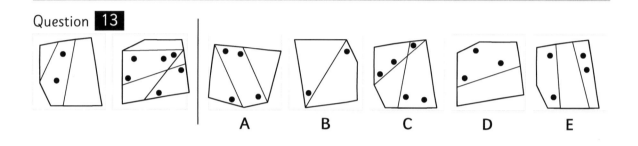

A      B      C      D      E

**Question 14**

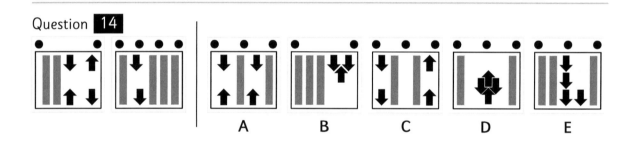

A      B      C      D      E

**Question 15**

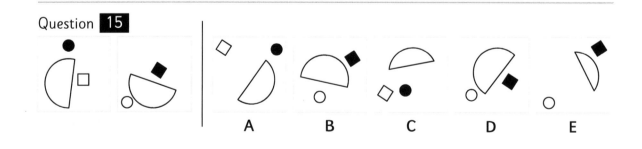

A      B      C      D      E

# Answers to Session 4

In this session you may have noticed you have been practicing only simple principles, at the heart of the non-verbal reasoning: counting and rotation. Full training in these is given in the extensive graded practice of sequences in Book 1 of the Non-Verbal Ninja Training Course.

---

Answer **1**

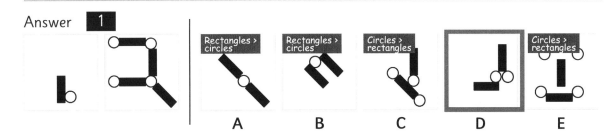

The rule is that there must be an equal number of circles and black rectangles.

---

Answer **2**

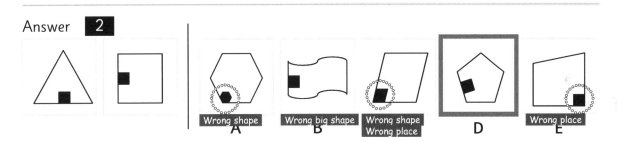

The pattern is a shape with a certain number of equal-length sides and equal angles, which has midway along one of its sides a black square intruding into it.

---

Answer **3**

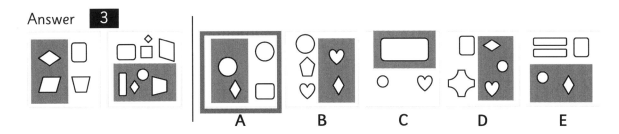

In each cell in the group, there are the same number of items inside the grey shape as outside it. It does not matter what those shapes are: they can be repeated.

---

Go to the next page ➡

Answer ⬛4

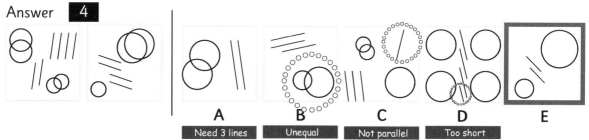

A — Need 3 lines
B — Unequal
C — Not parallel
D — Too short
E

The number of regions in the circles (counting each overlap zone as an extra region) equals the number of lines. The circles have different sizes but all pairs of overlapping circles are two circles of the same size. Within each cell all lines are the same size and parallel.

Answer ⬛5

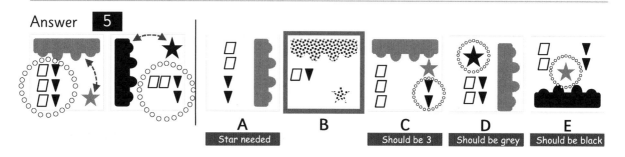

A — Star needed
B
C — Should be 3
D — Should be grey
E — Should be black

The star has to be the same colour as the large shape. The other small elements, white parallelograms and black triangles, have to be equal in number.

Answer ⬛6

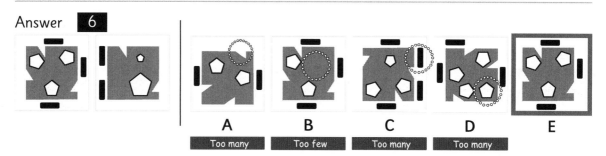

A — Too many
B — Too few
C — Too many
D — Too many
E

In each example shape, there is an equal number of black bars, pentagons, and triangular indentations of the grey shape. This number is 3 in the first example and 2 in the second. Only E follows this rule.

Answer ⬛7

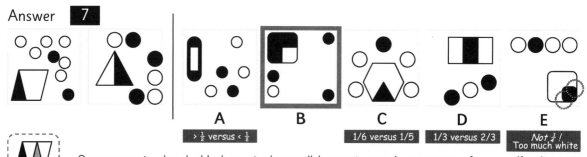

A — > ½ versus < ½
B
C — 1/6 versus 1/5
D — 1/3 versus 2/3
E — Not ¼ ! Too much white

Once you notice that the black part in the parallelogram is *exactly* one-quarter of its area (for the reason shown in the sketch on the left), you should check the proportion of circles that are black: this is 2/8 or ¼, too. The same pattern holds for the second cell: ½ of the triangle, and of the circles 3/6=½.

Go to the next page ➡

Answer 8

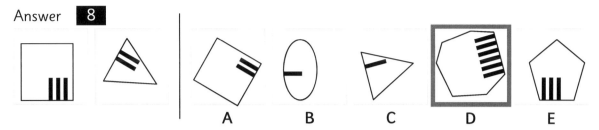

The outer shape is marked by a number of identical short thick black lines. The number of lines is one less than the number of sides of the outer shape. In the example cells, there are 4 sides and 3 lines, and then 3 sides and two lines. D fits the pattern, with 7 sides and 6 lines.

Answer 9

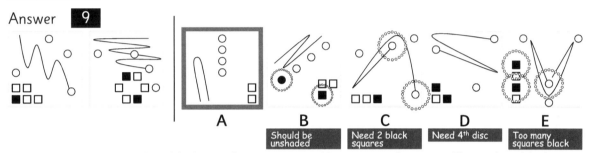

There is a curve with a number of fairly straight segments joined by very curved segments. The number of fairly straight segments matches the number of squares: 5 and 6 respectively. The number of squares that are shaded black is equal to the number of discs covering part of the curve. There are 4 discs in total, all unshaded.

Answer 10

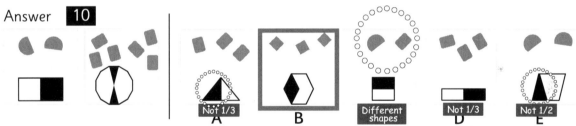

At the top of each cell is a number of grey elements, identical to each other but at different angles. However many of these elements there are, let's call it $n$, a fraction of $1/n$ of the lower shape is shaded black. In the first example, it is 2 and ½. In the second, 5 and 1/5 (drawn as 2 out of 10 segments in a 10-sided shape since 2/10 = 1/5 ).

B fits this rule since shading 2 segments of a hexagon gives 2/6 = 1/3.

Answer 11

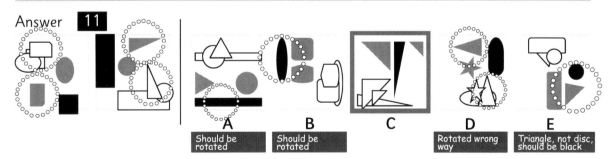

Each cell contains three elements appearing twice. One set is as three overlapping outline elements. These appear again in the cell, not overlapped but rotated 90 degrees clockwise (see the highlighted objects for confirmation); whichever element was at the back in the overlapped set, is now black, with the others grey.

Go to the next page ➡

Answer **12**

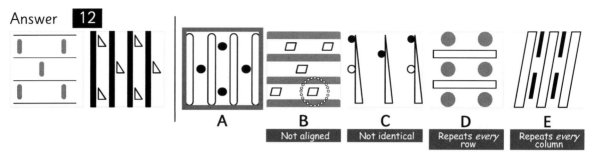

| A | B | C | D | E |
|---|---|---|---|---|
| | Not aligned | Not identical | Repeats *every* row | Repeats *every* column |

The theme is a series of parallel, identical bars or lines (vertical or horizontal), separated by small, repeating, identical elements. The pattern of small separator elements repeats, after two units, i.e. the third is like the first, and so on. If A was not available, you would choose B. But with A available its alignment provides a stronger rule than B.

Answer **13**

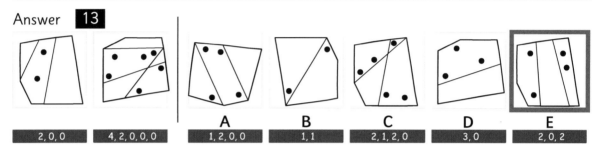

| 2, 0, 0 | 4, 2, 0, 0, 0 | A 1, 2, 0, 0 | B 1, 1 | C 2, 1, 2, 0 | D 3, 0 | E 2, 0, 2 |
|---|---|---|---|---|---|---|

If you jot down the number of dots in each piece of the shape (the order of numbers doesn't matter) as shown above, you will see the pattern very easily. All the numbers are even in the example cells. Only E matches this.

Answer **14**

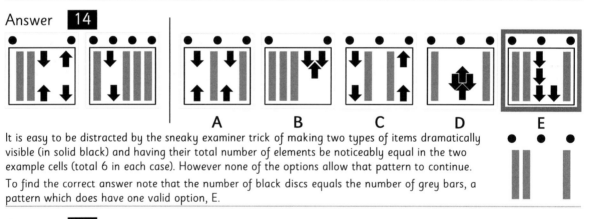

It is easy to be distracted by the sneaky examiner trick of making two types of items dramatically visible (in solid black) and having their total number of elements be noticeably equal in the two example cells (total 6 in each case). However none of the options allow that pattern to continue.

To find the correct answer note that the number of black discs equals the number of grey bars, a pattern which does have one valid option, E.

Answer **15**

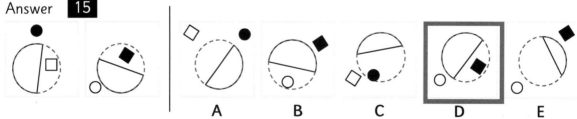

| A | B | C | D | E |
|---|---|---|---|---|

All the options have a large element which is part of a disc. They all have a small disc and a small square, one of which is black. It can't be the colour of the small elements as both colour schemes are present.

To find the answer, try to imagine the whole disc (shown here with dotted lines). You can see that the two question cells have the square inside the imaginary completed disc, and only one of the answer options fits this rule.

# Training Session 5

Now we move on to more advanced detection of groups. You will need your full repertoire of ninja skills from the Non-Verbal Ninja Training Course so far. But even those will not be enough because there are some new rules: be prepared to think laterally.

Question **1**

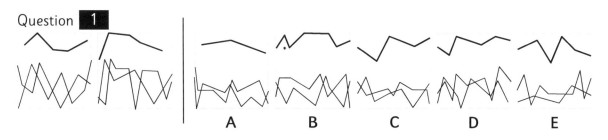

This is a new rule within the training course. Don't get cross about how difficult this is!

Question **2**

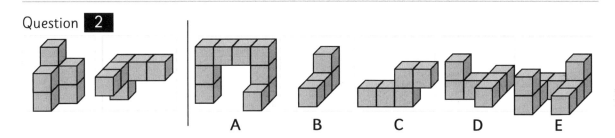

When faced with a difficult problem, try to look at it from different angles!

Question **3**

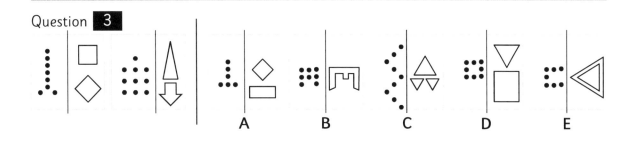

Go to the next page ➡

Question **4**

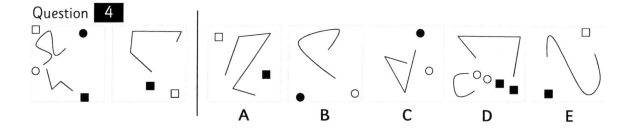

A          B          C          D          E

Question **5**

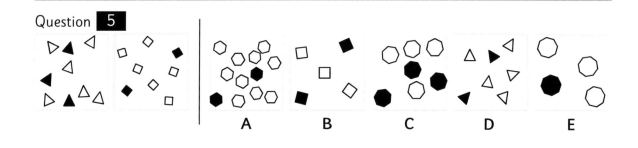

A          B          C          D          E

Question **6**

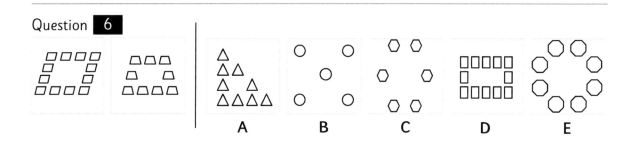

A          B          C          D          E

Question **7**

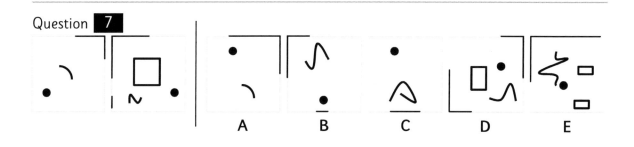

A          B          C          D          E

## Question 8

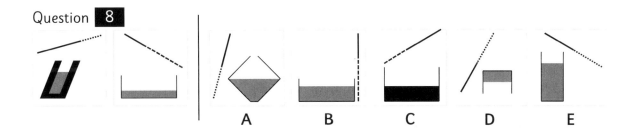

A     B     C     D     E

## Question 9

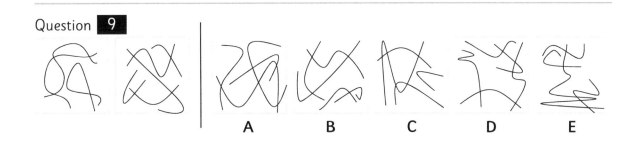

A     B     C     D     E

## Question 10

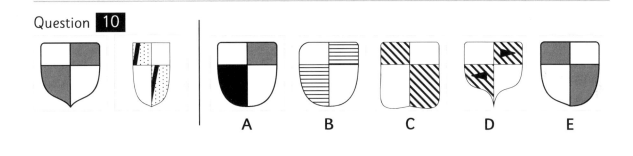

A     B     C     D     E

## Question 11

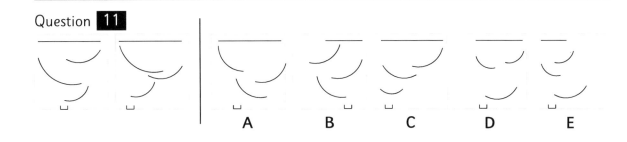

A     B     C     D     E

Go to the next page

## Question 12

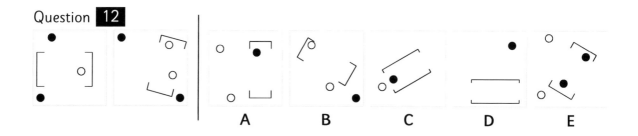

A     B     C     D     E

## Question 13

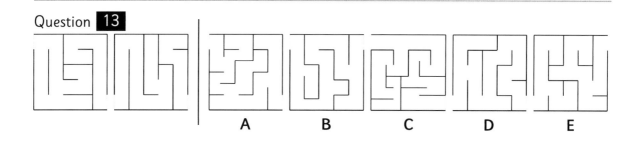

A     B     C     D     E

## Question 14

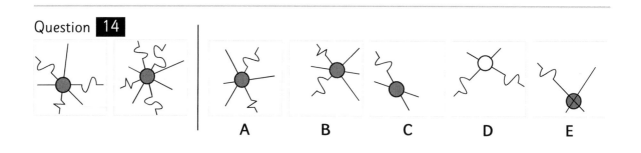

A     B     C     D     E

## Question 15

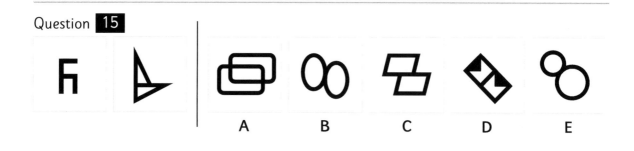

A     B     C     D     E

Go to the next page

# Answers to Session 5

Look carefully at the explanations. Even if you chose the right answer by chance, it is important to understand the reasoning behind the question. You might have found a rule that suggested another option, but (a) did that rule only select a single option and (b) is it simpler than the rule described in the answers?

Examiners like rules that are simple, even if the rules are not obvious until explained!

Answer **1**

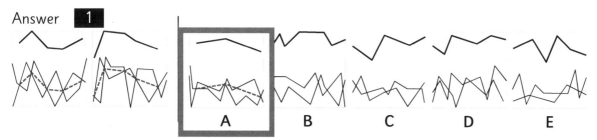

When you see a higgledy piggledy set of lines crossing over each other, remember to look at where they **cross**. The thick line at the top shows the course of the crossing points of the two lines in the lower part of the cell (which we have highlighted with dotted lines here).

Answer **2**

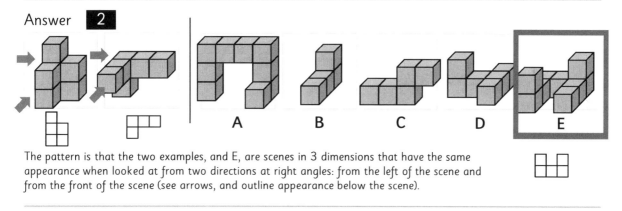

The pattern is that the two examples, and E, are scenes in 3 dimensions that have the same appearance when looked at from two directions at right angles: from the left of the scene and from the front of the scene (see arrows, and outline appearance below the scene).

Answer **3**

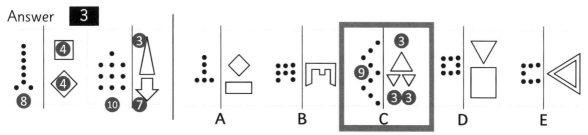

The total number of sides of the shapes on the right equals the number of dots on the left.

Go to the next page

## Answer 4

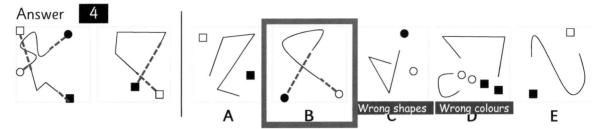

Beyond the ends of the smooth curve, in a straight line extended from the outer ends of the curve (as shown by the dotted line) is one unshaded circle and one black-shaded circle. Similarly, for the shapes made of straight line segments (rather than curves), there is an unshaded square and a black-shaded square.

## Answer 5

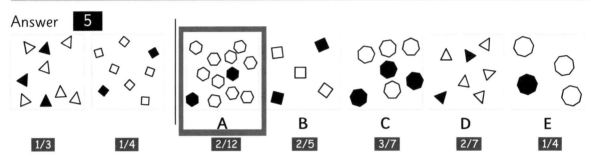

In the cell with 3-sided shapes, 1/**3** of them are shaded black. In the cell with 4-sided elements, 1/**4** of them are shaded black. A, with **6**-sided elements, has 2/12=1/**6** of them shaded black.

## Answer 6

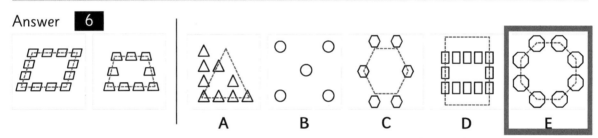

The elements are arranged in a shape which draws out an enlarged version of one element. The enlarged version must be scaled appropriately, not skewed (tilted) like A or stretched in one direction like C and D.

## Answer 7

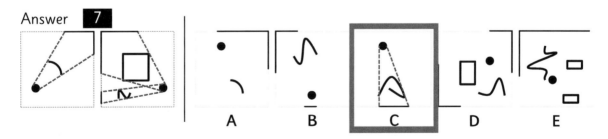

Imagine light coming out of the black disc, and illuminating the other element or element near the disc: a shadow would be cast. The straight lines show the shadow. Only in C does the straight line show the shadow of all the shapes in the cell.

## Answer 8

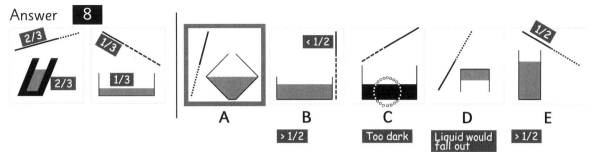

The large element is a container partially filled with grey liquid, at the bottom of the container. There is also a straight line that is partly solid and partly dotted. The proportion of the container that is filled with liquid equals the proportion of the line that is solid rather than dotted.

## Answer 9

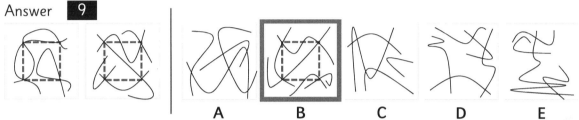

When there are lines, straight or curved, without an apparent pattern, look at their crossing points. In the examples, the crossing points form the corners of a square. Only B fits this rule.

## Answer 10

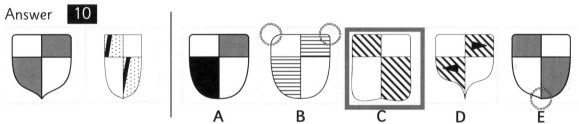

The design is symmetrical in outline, with four quadrants. The top left and bottom left quadrants have the same shading, with the pattern retaining the same orientation (direction), as seen in the second example. Likewise the top right and bottom left quadrants are similar.

This means D, whose triangle pattern is mirrored left/right between the top right and bottom left, does not fit the rule. B and E do not have symmetrical outlines.

## Answer 11

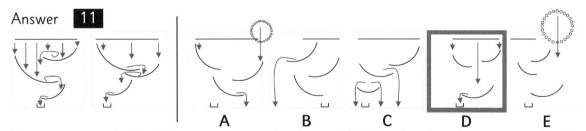

The curves represent bowls which can capture water dropping vertically. Water from the entire range spanned by the upper horizontal line (and no other water) will fall progressively from bowl to bowl until it reaches the rectangular tray at the bottom. In A and E the upper horizontal line is not wide enough to cover all the bowls.

Go to the next page ➡

## Answer 12

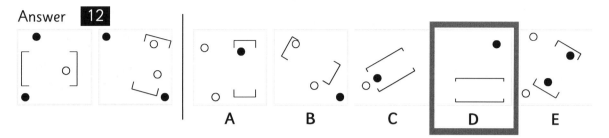

Inside the box whose corners are formed by the two square-bracket symbols, any circles are unfilled. Outside this box, any circles are filled in black.

## Answer 13

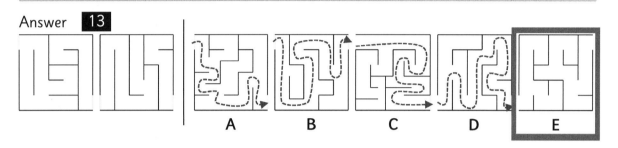

The examples are mazes with no paths from left to right. All the options have a path from left to right, except E.

## Answer 14

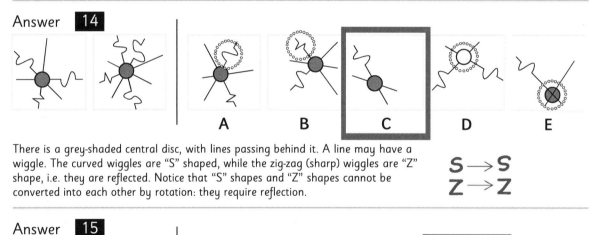

There is a grey-shaded central disc, with lines passing behind it. A line may have a wiggle. The curved wiggles are "S" shaped, while the zig-zag (sharp) wiggles are "Z" shape, i.e. they are reflected. Notice that "S" shapes and "Z" shapes cannot be converted into each other by rotation: they require reflection.

$$S \rightarrow S$$
$$Z \rightarrow Z$$

## Answer 15

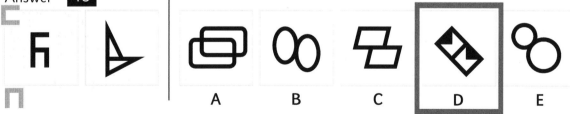

The design consists of two copies of the same element. One copy is rotated anticlockwise but not changed in size. Their edges overlap. Near the first cell we have drawn non-overlapped copies of the element so the rotation can be more easily seen.

Go to the next page ➡

# Training Session 6

Question **1**

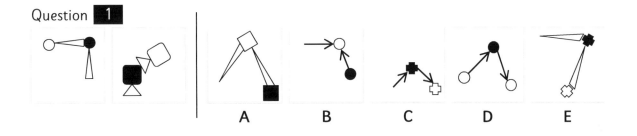

A     B     C     D     E

Question **2**

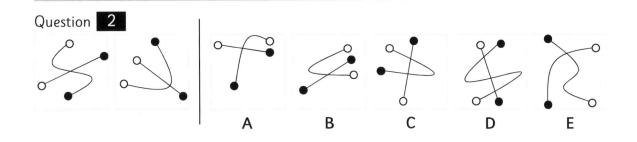

A     B     C     D     E

Question **3**

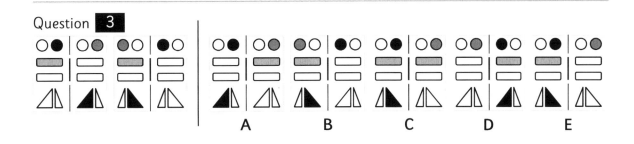

A     B     C     D     E

Go to the next page

## Question 4

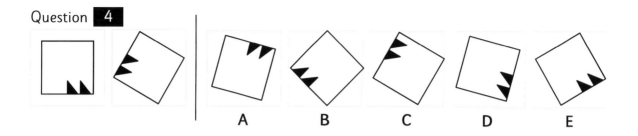

A  B  C  D  E

## Question 5

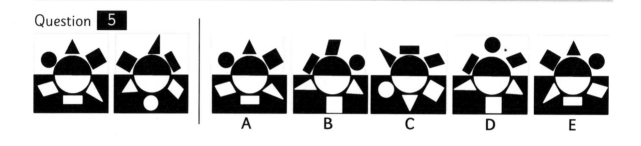

A  B  C  D  E

## Question 6

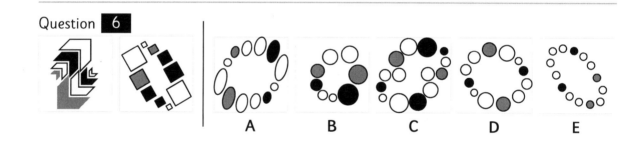

A  B  C  D  E

## Question 7

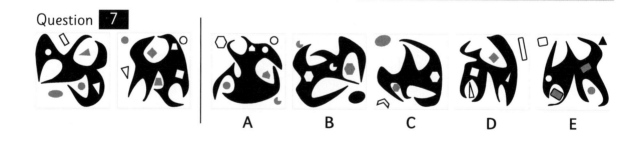

A  B  C  D  E

Go to the next page

## Question

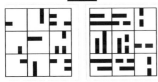    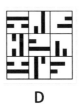 

A       B       C       D       E

## Question 9

A       B       C       D       E

## Question 10

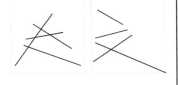     

A       B       C       D       E

## Question 11

A       B       C       D       E

## Question 12

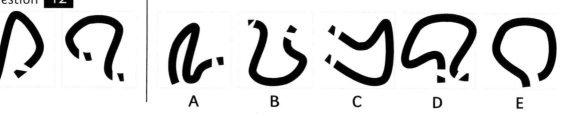

A    B    C    D    E

## Question 13

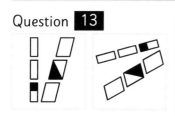
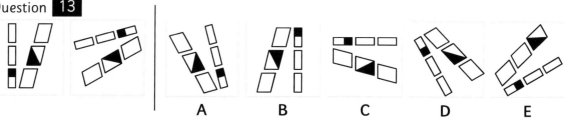

A    B    C    D    E

## Question 14

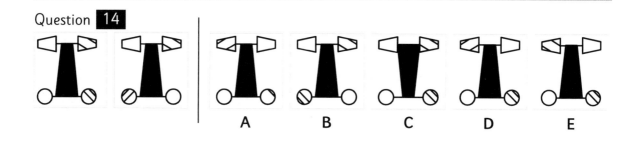

A    B    C    D    E

## Question 15

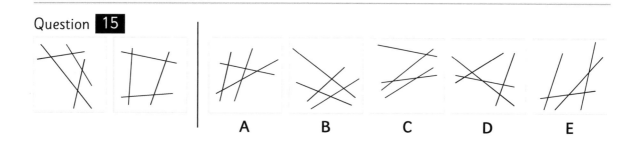

A    B    C    D    E

# Answers to Session 6

Answer **1**

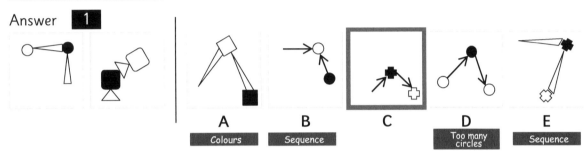

There are two identical pointed structures (which we can call arrows) and two identical (although one is shaded black) non-pointed structures. Reading in the direction of the arrows, the sequence is: arrow, black non-pointed, arrow, unshaded non-pointed.

Answer **2**

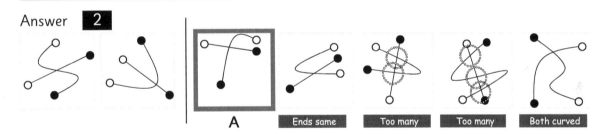

There is one straight line and one curved line. They cross at a single point. Each line has an unfilled circle at one end and a black-filled circle at the other end.

Answer **3**

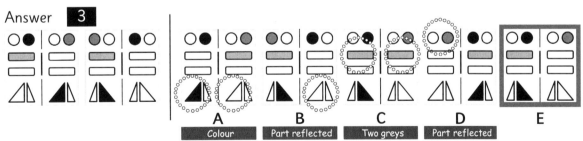

The design contains three levels: top, middle and bottom. Each one is allowed to reflect, but if reflecting the whole level must reflect (not just the left or right part). The examples do not show the middle level reflecting, and you might suspect that the thick line means "cannot reflect", but it doesn't matter as the correct answer does not require the middle level to reflect.

Go to the next page ➡

## Answer 4

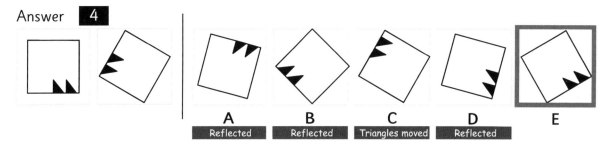

A — Reflected
B — Reflected
C — Triangles moved
D — Reflected
E

The two examples and the correct answer are all pure rotations of each other.

## Answer 5

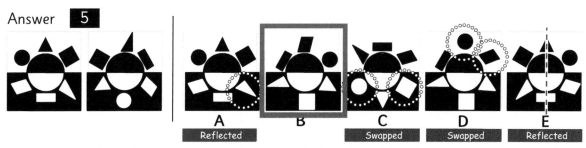

A — Reflected
B
C — Swapped
D — Swapped
E — Reflected

There is a central disc and six elements arranged around it. The lower half of the cell is reversed in colour, with that part of the disc and the whole of the smaller elements in that region shaded white on a black background. The group of six elements appears in two different rotated – but not reflected – orientations in the examples.

## Answer 6

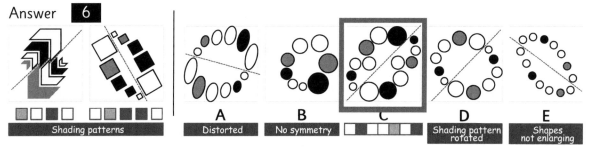

Shading patterns

A — Distorted
B — No symmetry
C
D — Shading pattern rotated
E — Shapes not enlarging

Each design is a series of elements increasing in size (without being distorted), arranged side-by-side, with the series repeated after a 180° rotation. The shading pattern is not rotated, however. It runs in the same direction for both copies rather than rotating with them, so that the overall design only has rotational symmetry if shading is ignored.

## Answer 7

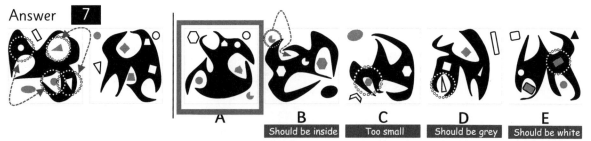

A
B — Should be inside
C — Too small
D — Should be grey
E — Should be white

There is a large, irregular black-shaded element which has prongs sticking out, sometimes enclosing a small element. The large element has some white elements embedded within it. Whenever the prongs enclose an element, the element is grey, and another copy of the element appears, coloured white, embedded in the black element. This pairing is shown in the first cell, as an example.

Go to the next page ➡

## Answer 8

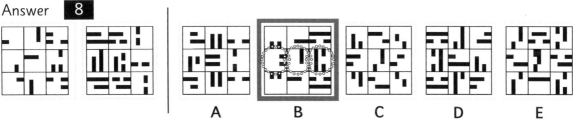

You will quickly notice that in each column within the cell, the three elements are rotated versions of each other (this is particularly obvious in the left column of the first example cell). More specifically, they rotate anticlockwise as your eye moves down the cell.

## Answer 9

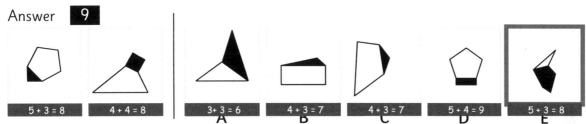

The two examples are of two polygons touching each other, with their touching sides being identical in length. One is shaded black and the other is unshaded. The total number of sides is 8.

## Answer 10

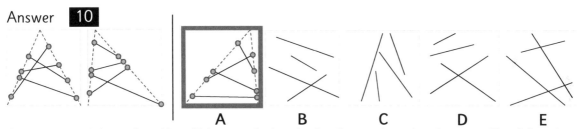

Once you discard the number of lines (4 for examples but also for all options), number of crossings (3 and 1), and number of regions enclosed (1 and 0), you must look for a different type of rule. If you highlight the ends of the lines (as shown above) you see that in both examples, the points at the left end of each line form a straight line (drawn dashed), as do the points at the right end of each line. This is a very unusual finding for four randomly drawn lines, so it is the rule.

## Answer 11

A quick way to realise that a complex, wiggly shape has been reflected rather than rotated is to pick an element which somewhat looks like an asymmetrical letter (here we think one element looks like a capital "L") and quickly write the "L" next to the letter in all the cells. This makes it obvious that several of the options are reflected. Do not use a symmetrical letter such as "M" or "Y", as you won't be able to detect a reflection, and don't write the "L" with equal-length arms.

Go to the next page ➡

Answer **12**

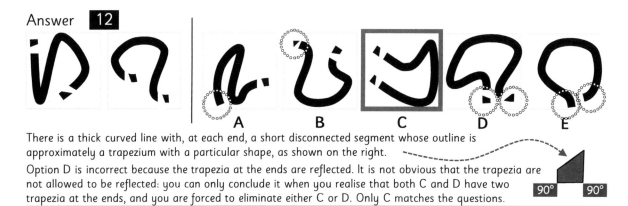

There is a thick curved line with, at each end, a short disconnected segment whose outline is approximately a trapezium with a particular shape, as shown on the right.

Option D is incorrect because the trapezia at the ends are reflected. It is not obvious that the trapezia are not allowed to be reflected: you can only conclude it when you realise that both C and D have two trapezia at the ends, and you are forced to eliminate either C or D. Only C matches the questions.

Answer **13**

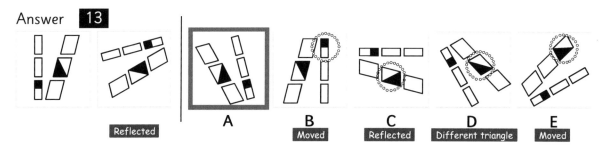

The two examples already show reflection of the entire shape, so reflection (of the entire shape) must be allowed in the rule. In D, a different triangle is shaded, using the long diagonal of the parallelogram rather than the short one.

Answer **14**

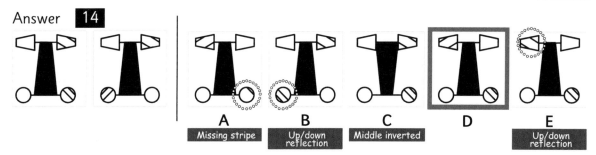

The design is a car-shape with two front wheels on an axle, and two rear wheels on an axle. The front section and rear section can each reflect left/right. You can deduce that they are not allowed to reflect up/down because if that was allowed, there would be multiple allowable answers, and yet you know there is only one allowable answer.

Answer **15**

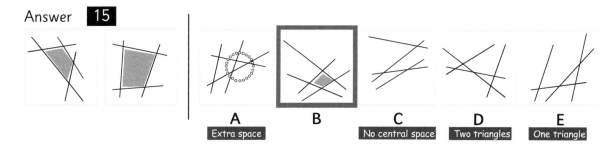

At first you might think that the rule is that there are 4 crossings, but this fits both B and E. Which one is more similar to the two examples? The answer is B, because there is a central space that is a quadrilateral.

Go to the next page ➡

# Training Session 7

You are now ready to graduate to advanced non-verbal ninja-training! We step up the learning level by asking you to identify **two** mystery cells in each 3x3 grid. This is more demanding, because you have less of a clue from the other cells.

However, this advanced training hones your ninja skills to the highest level. We will be using a wide array of rules in combination with each other, so keep your wits about you!

Questions **1, 2**

Draw a circle round your answer for question 1, and a double circle around your answer for question 2.

Questions **3, 4**

Questions **5, 6**

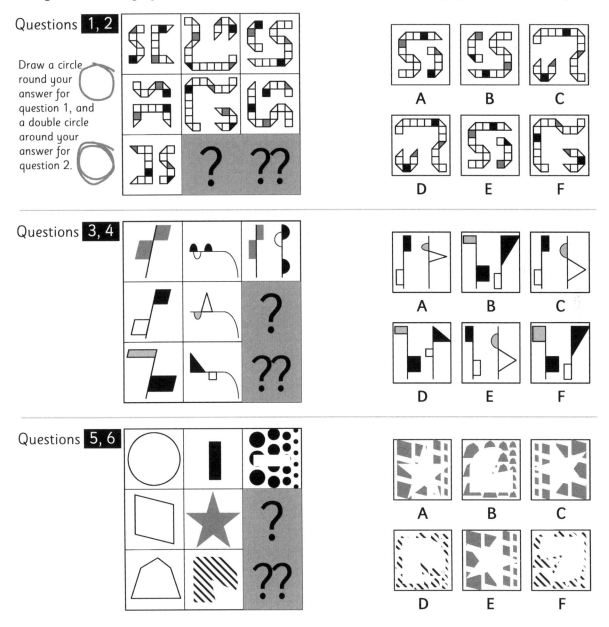

Go to the next page ➡

Questions **7, 8**

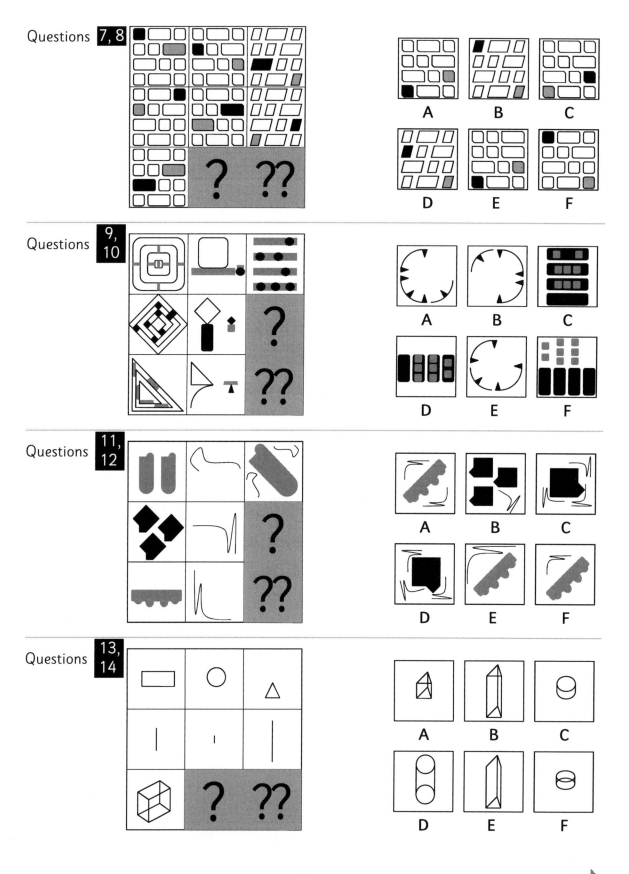

A   B   C

D   E   F

Questions **9, 10**

A   B   C

D   E   F

Questions **11, 12**

A   B   C

D   E   F

Questions **13, 14**

A   B   C

D   E   F

Go to the next page

Questions **15, 16**

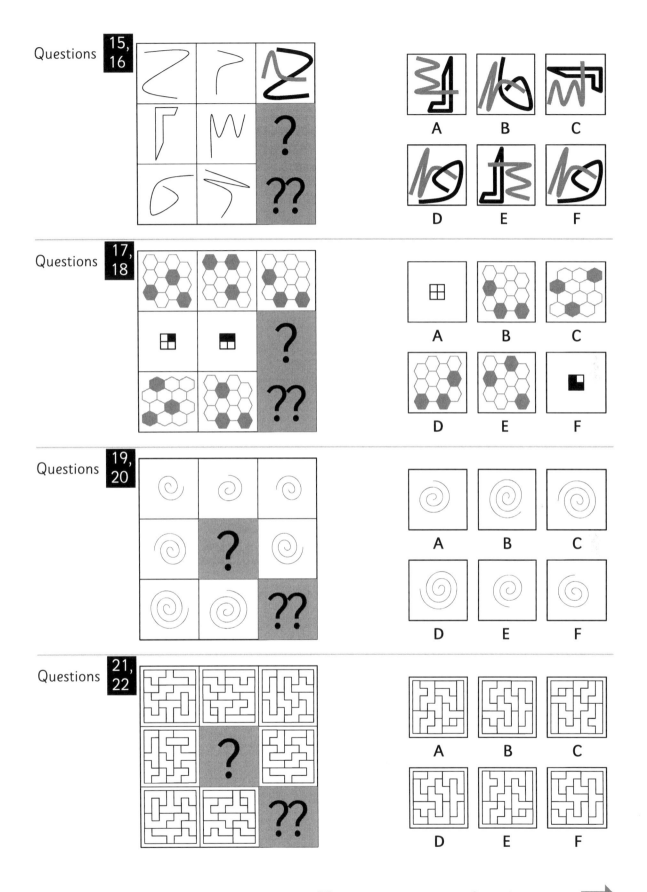

Questions **17, 18**

Questions **19, 20**

Questions **21, 22**

Questions **23, 24**

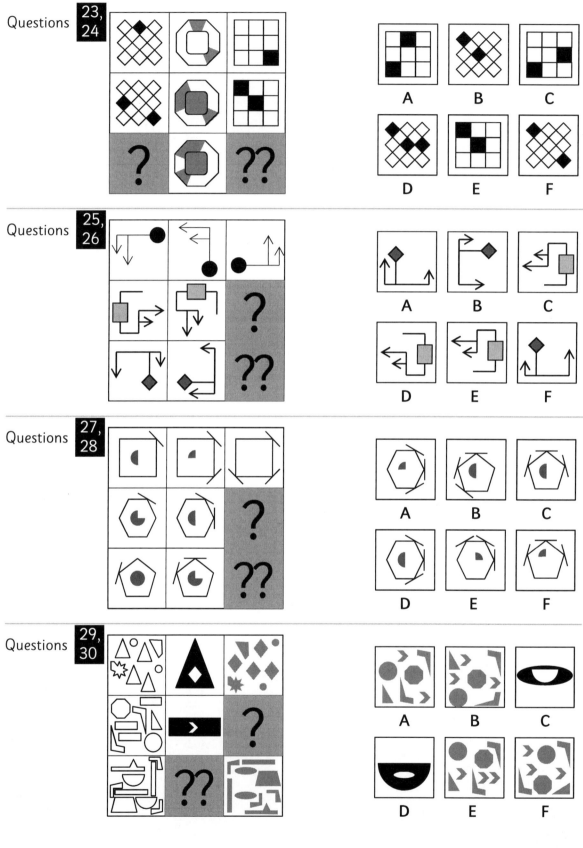

A  B  C
D  E  F

Questions **25, 26**

A  B  C
D  E  F

Questions **27, 28**

A  B  C
D  E  F

Questions **29, 30**

A  B  C
D  E  F

This is the end of this session.

# Answers to Session 7

In each pair of questions the answer to the first is given by a thick box as before, while the answer to the second is given as a thin double box.

## Answers 1, 2

As marked in the top left cell, from top to bottom in a column, the shading pattern moves in a circuit along each chain of squares and triangles. When a shading leaves the end of a chain, it

rejoins the chain at the other end. Meanwhile the entire design is rotating clockwise. Each column has a separate design.

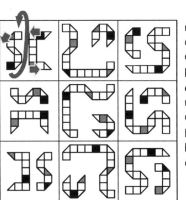

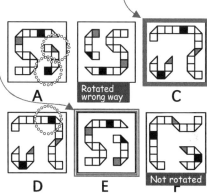

A

B — Rotated wrong way

C

D

E

F — Not rotated

## Answers 3, 4

In each row, the element in the left cell appears in the right cell, but with the sloping axis made vertical and the horizontal width of the flag shape reduced by half. The element in the middle cell appears

in the right cell, but with the "wilting" shape straightened and the vertical height of the resulting shape doubled.

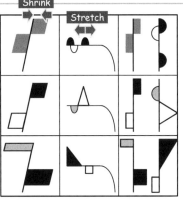

Shrink

Stretch

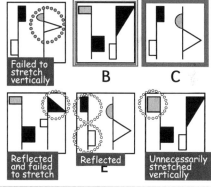

A — Failed to stretch vertically

B

C

D — Reflected and failed to stretch

E — Reflected

F — Unnecessarily stretched vertically

## Answers 5, 6

Copies of the left cell element, filled in the shading of the middle cell element, are duplicated at progressively smaller sizes from left to right in the right cell.

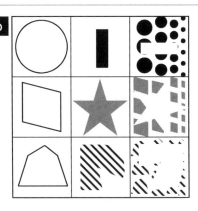

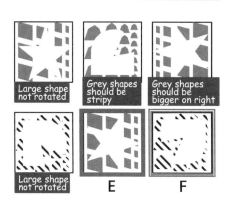

A — Large shape not rotated

B — Grey shapes should be stripy

C — Grey shapes should be bigger on right

D — Large shape not rotated

E

F

Go to the next page

## Answers 7, 8

In each column the framework of open shapes is constant between the three cells. In each row, the shading moves one step down from one cell to the next.

Although you are not shown that

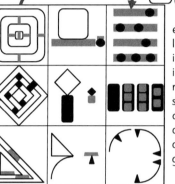

shading going off the bottom of a cell should reappear at the top, you know it should not appear in the second row (since that should match the previous top row)

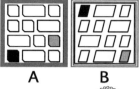

A  B  C

D  E  Wrong shapes

## Answers 9, 10

The central column explains how to convert the symbols in the left to those in the right. In the top row, for each rounded square on the left, a large horizontal grey bar is drawn, and for

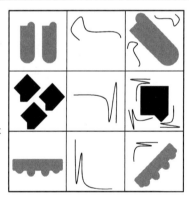

each small grey line immediately inside a rounded square, a black disc is drawn on the corresponding grey bar.

Too many   B   Black bars too long and rotated

D   2, 1, 2 is wrong order   The elements should be superimposed

## Answers 11, 12

In the left cell there are a certain number of copies (*n*) of an element. A single copy of that element appears in the right cell, rotated 45° anticlockwise and enlarged 50%.

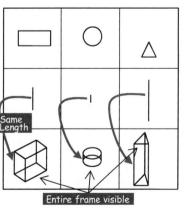

The squiggle in the middle cell is miniaturised (to half size) and appears *n* times (variously rotated) in the right cell.

Too many   B   Reflected

D   Not made smaller   F

## Answers 13, 14

The principle is simple: the shape in the top cell is drawn twice at an oblique 3-dimensional angle, one drawing above the other. These are joined by a suitable number of copies of the

Same Length

Entire frame visible

vertical line in the middle cell.

When you see that three options fit this simple rule, you must search out the two additional restrictions shown in the diagram.

Too short   B   Part of frame invisible

A   B   C

Too long   Part of frame invisible   F

D

Go to the next page ➡

## Answers 15, 16

In each row, the shape in the left cell is rotated 180° and thickened, to form the bottom layer of the right cell.

The shape in the middle cell is rotated 90° anticlockwise and

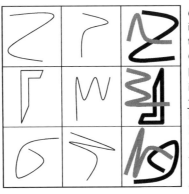

drawn thickly in grey, to form the upper layer of the right cell. D and F are identical except for their layering. So layering matters: choose the one that matches the top-right cell.

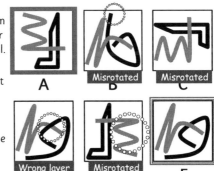

## Answers 17, 18

In each row, the number of quarters filled in black in the square in the middle cell, indicates how many quarter turns the top cell must be turned clockwise to make the bottom cell.

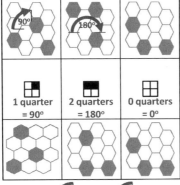

F is a dead end because if it is chosen there is no suitable choice for the second unknown cell.

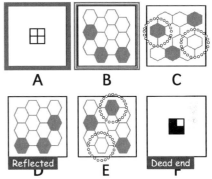

## Answers 19, 20

Examine the left column. Each row down adds a new 180° segment of spiral (highlighted with dashes).

Along each row, meanwhile, the designs rotate anticlockwise 90°.

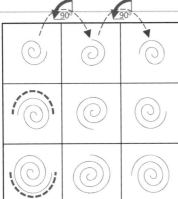

## Answers 21, 22

In each column, the design rotates anticlockwise 90° from top to bottom.

Tip: Draw the direction onto the page.

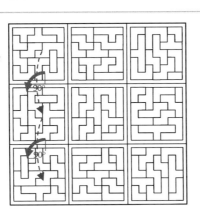
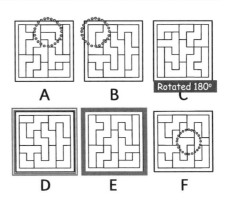

Go to the next page

## Answers 23, 24

In each row, there are three 3 x 3 grids. The central cell has elements filled in whenever the corresponding element in the left or right cell is filled. The grid parts are numbered here for easy

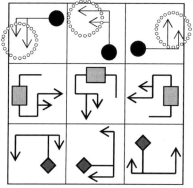

recognition:

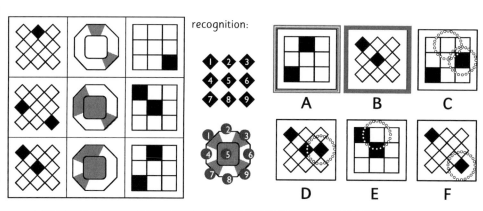

## Answers 25, 26

In each column, the design rotates clockwise *but* additionally the two arrows (short and long) exchange places.

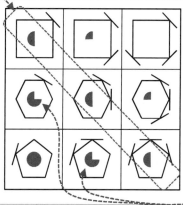

Arrows not swapped · Rotated · C

Reflected · Arrows not swapped · F

## Answers 27, 28

In each row, with each move to the right, the outer element gains an extra line at the next corner clockwise.

Along the top-left to bottom-right diagonals (one of which is marked

with a box) the central element is constant.

To choose between A and E, note that the central element doesn't rotate along this diagonal.

A · Wrong place B · C

Should be quarter-disc · Rotated E · Should be half-disc

## Answers 29, 30

In each row, the left cell is converted into the right cell by shading the elements grey and replacing the element shown (expanded) in the outer position of the middle cell

with the inner shape of the middle cell. Numbers and *orientations* are kept constant, although the positions are changed.

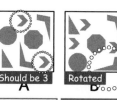

Should be 3 A · Rotated B · Wrong way round

D · E · Rotated F

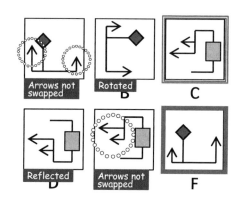

60   This is the end of this session. ⊗

# Training Session 8

You are progressing well in training in the Matrix type of Non-Verbal Reasoning question, young ninja!

Keep your mind open to looking for new types of rule, as well as combinations of rules that you are already expert in using.

Questions **1, 2**

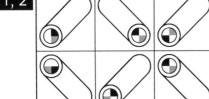

A　　　　B　　　　C

D　　　　E　　　　F

Questions **3, 4**

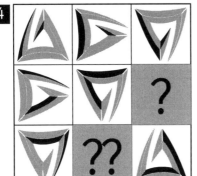

A　　　　B　　　　C

D　　　　E　　　　F

Questions **5, 6**

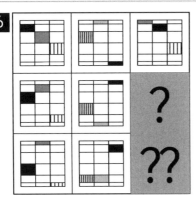

A　　　　B　　　　C

D　　　　E　　　　F

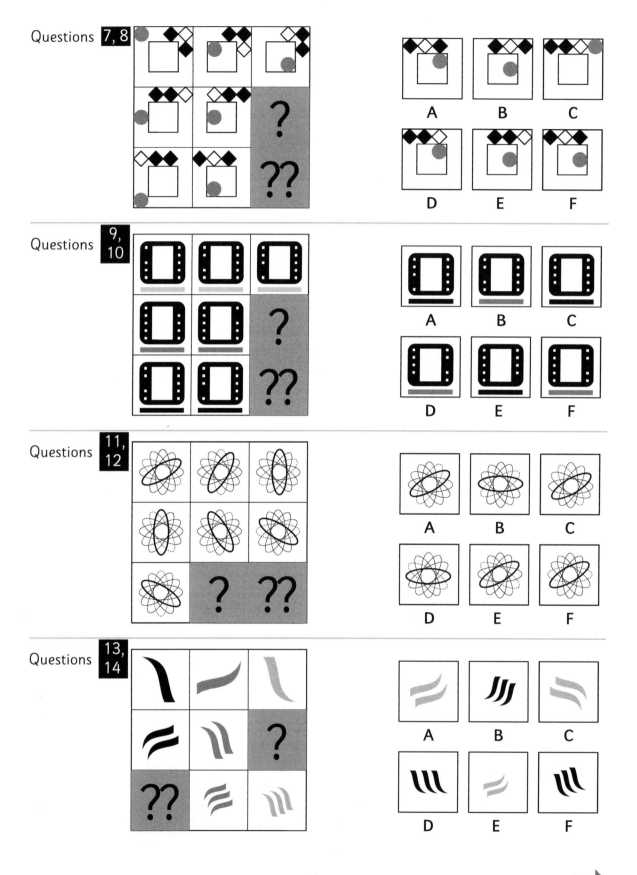

Questions **7, 8**

Questions **9, 10**

Questions **11, 12**

Questions **13, 14**

Questions 15, 16

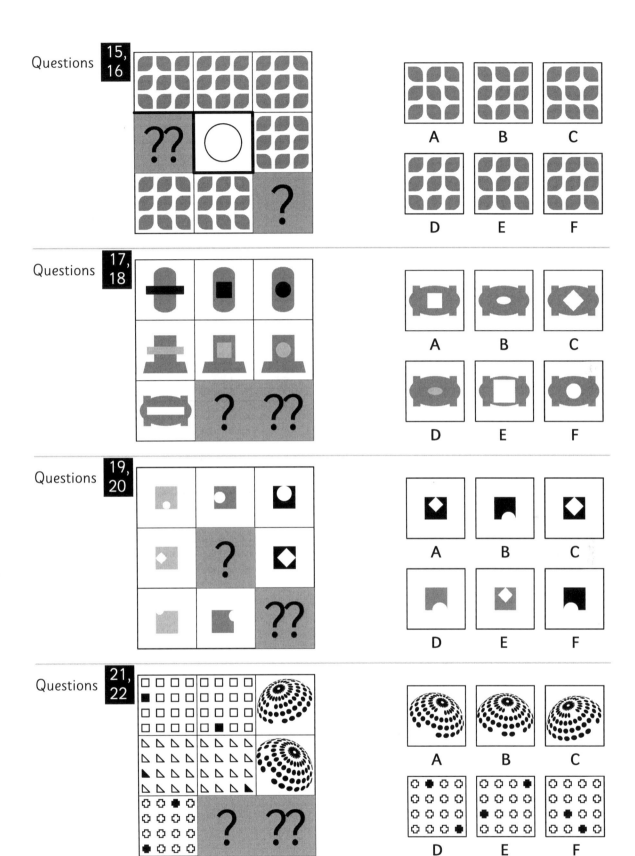

Questions 17, 18

Questions 19, 20

Questions 21, 22

Go to the next page

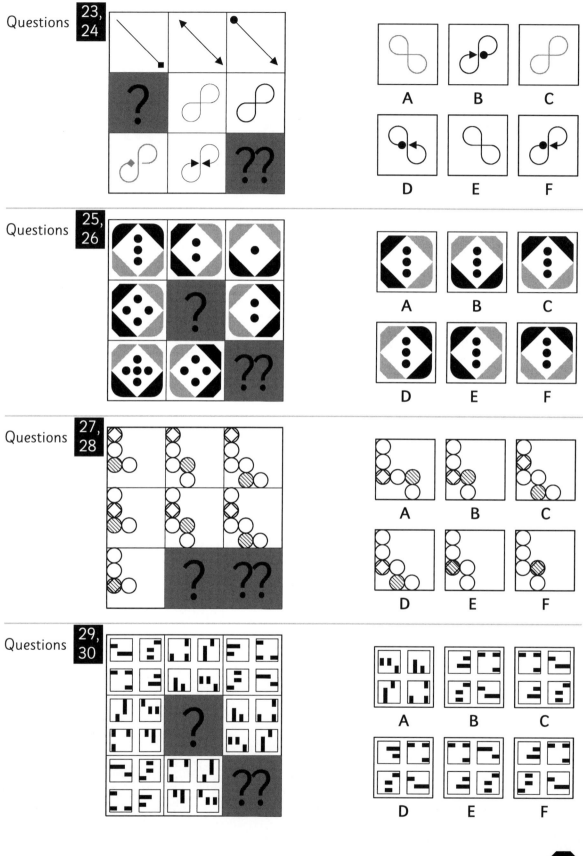

Questions 23, 24

Questions 25, 26

Questions 27, 28

Questions 29, 30

64

This is the end of this session.

# Answers to Session 8

Tackling these advanced questions gives you advanced ninja skills. Do not be disappointed if you found many of these difficult. Your ninja trainers have selected each question to be difficult to some young ninjas, so the learning points come thick and fast.

Remember that the real exam will have a mixture of easy questions (for everyone to get right) and hard ones for which this course is preparing you.

## Answers 1, 2

In each column (the left column is highlighted as an example), the entire design rotates clockwise, taking with it the black and grey markings in the small disc.

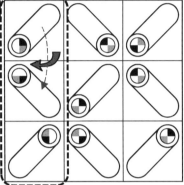

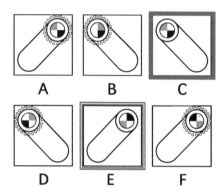

## Answers 3, 4

The design rotates clockwise one step with every move to the right or down.

In the top row the inner black shading is always at the innermost segment among the inner segments; it moves to the next

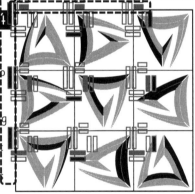

segment in the second row and third in the third row.

In the left column the outer black shading is at the outermost segment. It moves along in the other columns.

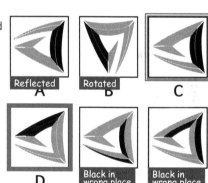

## Answers 5, 6

Each of the 9 cells contains 3 columns of rectangles. From one cell to the cell below, the shading pattern moves vertically one position (shown by straight arrows): downwards in the left column,

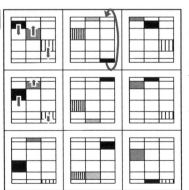

upwards in the middle column and downwards in the right column.

Shading going out of one end of a column rejoins at the other end of the column (curved arrow).

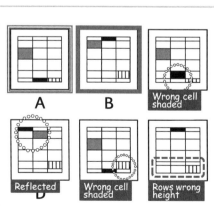

Go to the next page

## Answers 7, 8

The grey disc moves downward with every descent to a lower row. With every column to the right, the grey disc moves towards (or past) the centre of the cell.

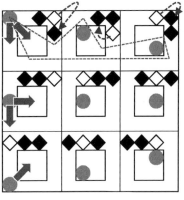

The chain of diamonds moves anticlockwise one step for each step down one row. The shading pattern moves clockwise with each column right.

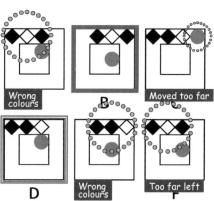

Wrong colours
B
Moved too far
D
Wrong colours
Too far left

## Answers 9, 10

In each row, the shading of the bar at the bottom of the cell is constant. From left to right, the gap in the grid of white spots moves down one position.

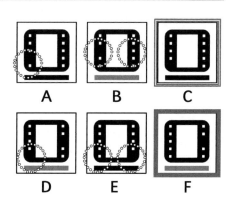

A    B    C

D    E    F

## Answers 11, 12

The *thick* marking of one ellipse moves one step anticlockwise along a row and two steps anticlockwise along each column.

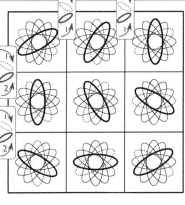

The *dashed* marking of one ellipse moves two steps clockwise along each row and one step clockwise along each column.

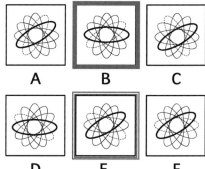

A    B    C

D    E    F

## Answers 13, 14

From left to right the shading becomes paler.

From top to bottom the design shrinks and rotates anticlockwise 90°, and the number of elements increases by 1.

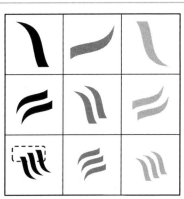

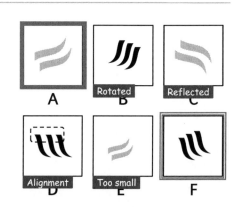

A    Rotated    Reflected

Alignment    Too small    F

Go to the next page

## Answers 15, 16

"Thinking around the box"

In this difficult question, in each step clockwise (starting from top left where the black line indicates a break in the sequence), one element – the one

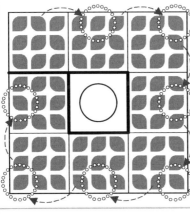

which indicates the position of the present cell in relation to the entire matrix of cells – is reflected.

If you circle the changes, the pattern is easy to see.

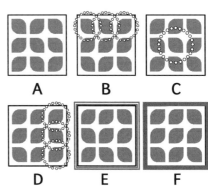

A    B    C

D    E    F

## Answers 17, 18

In each row, the background grey element is common to all three cells.

In each column, the foreground element (highlighted with dashes in the left column) becomes progressively lighter in colour

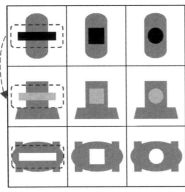

from top to bottom.

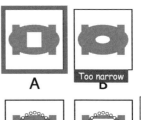

A    B    C
Too narrow    Rotated

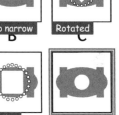

Too dark
Too narrow    Too big    F
        E

## Answers 19, 20

In each row, from left to right the central shape rotates clockwise 90°, with the outer region becoming darker and the inner region growing in size.

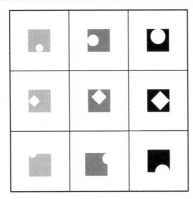

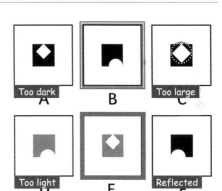

A    B    C
Too dark        Too large

D    E    F
Too light        Reflected

## Answers 21, 22

In each row, the left and middle cells indicate **relative** grid positions that are coloured differently (black): in the right cell, elements in those **relative** positions are missing, as shown in the sketches on the right.

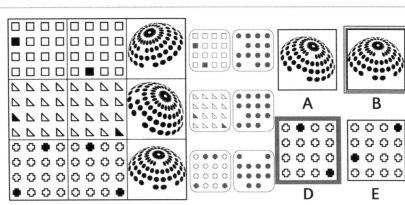

A    B    C

D    E    F

Go to the next page

Answers

In each column, the bottom cell is drawn in the line thickness and colour of the middle cell.

The line in the top cell tells us whether arrowheads or other line endings should be drawn

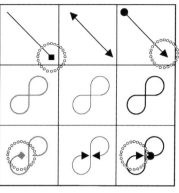

on the design in the bottom cell.

The first column shows that the **right** end of the line in the top cell tells us what ending to put on the **left** end of the line in the bottom cell.

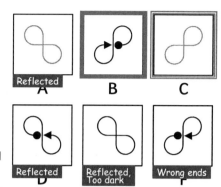

Answers 25, 26

The outer *shape*

is rounded on two sides and sharp on the other two. It rotates *clockwise* in each row and each column.

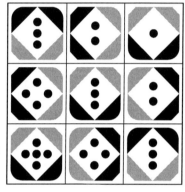

Meanwhile the *shading* pattern

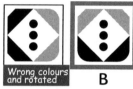

rotates *anticlockwise* in each row and each column.

The number of dots increases diagonally from top right.

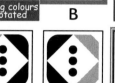

Answers 27, 28

Within each row, each step to the right adds another circle to the end of the chain of circles.

The circle one step away from the growing end of the chain is shaded.

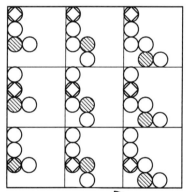

Within each column, the position of the diamond-shaped mark moves down one position with each step down.

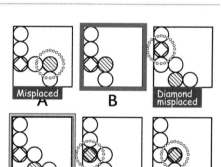

Answers 29, 30

Within each column, from top to bottom the four elements in each cell rotate anticlockwise 90°. (As an example, one element is highlighted on the left.)

Within each row, from left to right the entire design rotates clockwise 90°. (As an example, two cells are highlighted at the top.)

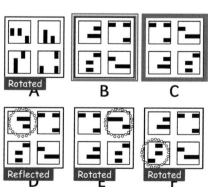

This is the end of this session. ✖

# Training Session 9

You are now at the advanced level of non-verbal ninja!
Expect all kinds of anything, at any time, and in any combination.

Ready?

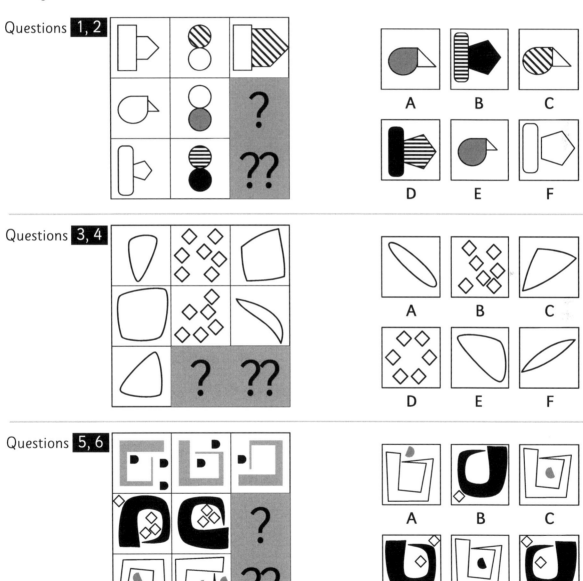

Questions 1, 2

Questions 3, 4

Questions 5, 6

Go to the next page

Questions **7, 8**

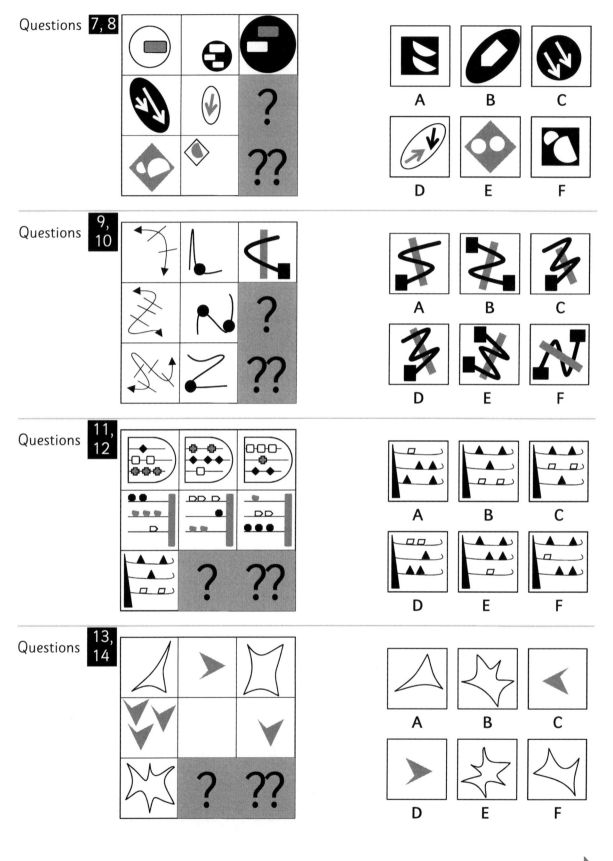

Questions **9, 10**

Questions **11, 12**

Questions **13, 14**

Go to the next page ➡

Questions **15, 16**

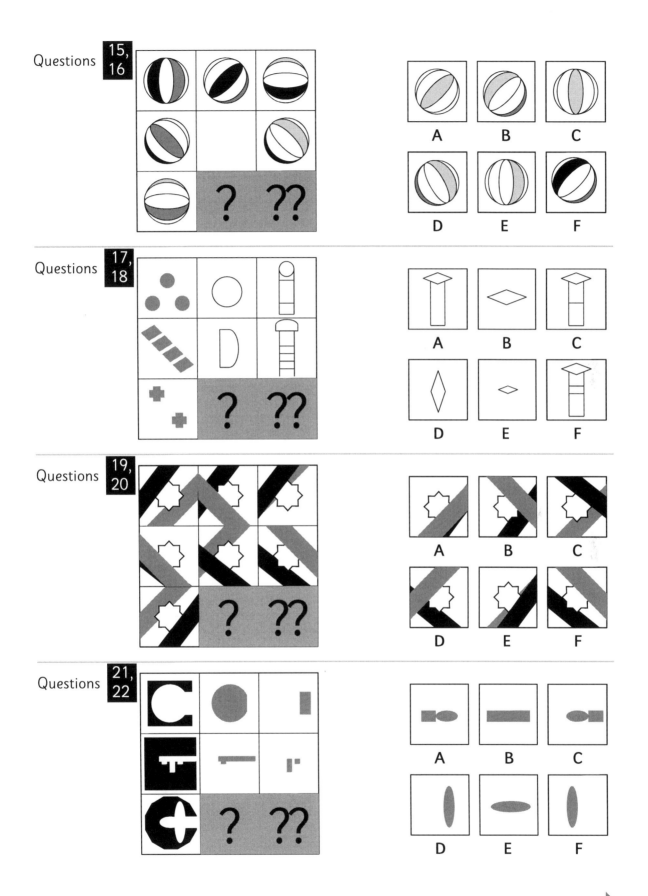

Questions **17, 18**

Questions **19, 20**

Questions **21, 22**

Go to the next page

Questions **23, 24**

Questions **25, 26**

Questions **27, 28**

Questions **29, 30**

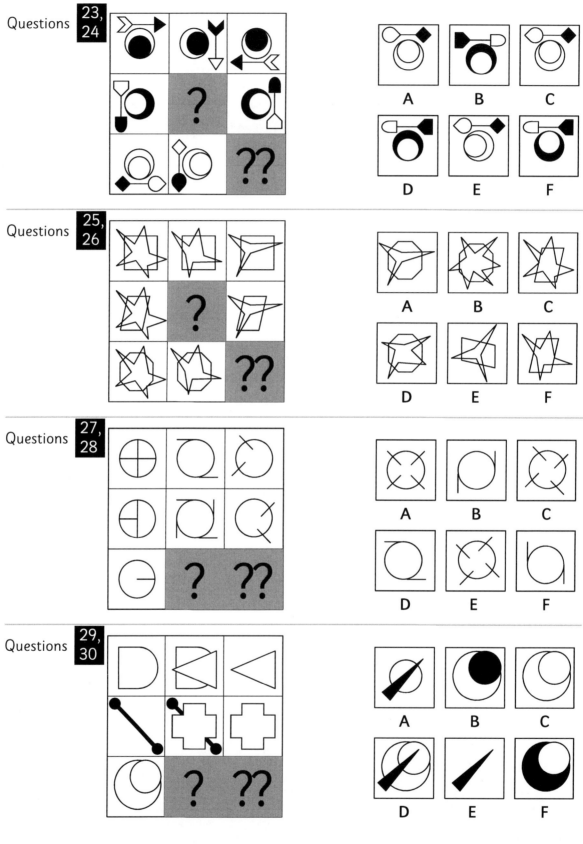

A B C

D E F

72

This is the end of this session. ✖

You might have found quite a few challenging questions in this session.

Success in exams comes from practicing problems that stretch and extend your skills, not just easy ones. Examine the explanations carefully to maximise your learning.

Answers **1, 2**

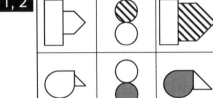
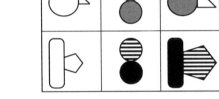

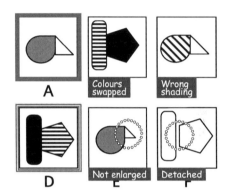

Answers **3, 4**

The left column contains rounded polygons with rounded corners, while the right column contains rounded polygons with pointed corners.

The middle column contains a number

of elements which matches the sum of the number of sides (or corners) of the elements in the left and right cells.

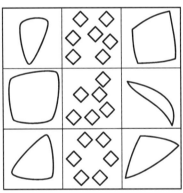

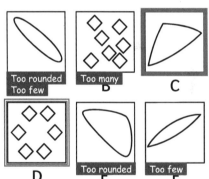

Answers **5, 6**

In each row, a large outer element rotates anticlockwise. There are also small elements which reduce in number by 1, but do not change their orientation.

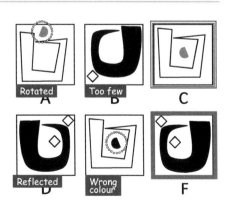

Go to the next page

## Answers 7, 8

Each row contains one type of element in another type of element: both types remain consistent across that row.

The top row shows that there can be

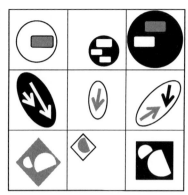

changes in:
• the numbers of small elements
• their colour
• their size

The middle row shows orientation can change.

Shapes changed

Shape changed

Outer shape changed

D

Shapes changed

F

## Answers 9, 10

In each row, the right cell contains a grey bar crossed by a black curve, the number of times given by the number of crossings of the curve in the left cell.

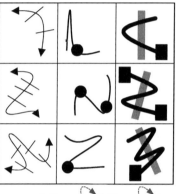

Moreover, the black curve has 1 or 2 blocks at its ends, determined by the number of black disks in the middle cell.

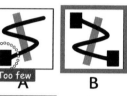
Too few — A

B

Too few crossings

D

Too many

Wrong layer

## Answers 11, 12

In each row, the type of element is moving downwards (as shown in the top row), while the number of elements is moving upwards (as shown in the top row).

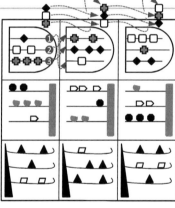

You can summarise the shapes and counts as shown below:

A

B

C

D

E

F

## Answers 13, 14

Following round the perimeter of the matrix along the direction of a cell with one or more grey arrows, every step from a corner to an adjacent corner increases the number of vertices

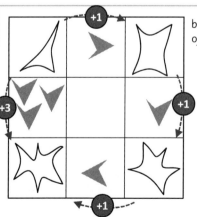

by the number of grey arrows.

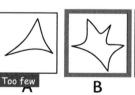
Too few — A

B

C

Reflected — D

Too many — E

Too few — F

Go to the next page ➡

## Answers 15, 16

At each step around the grid, the design rotates clockwise 45°. At the same time, the shading pattern moves across its surface in the direction shown by the arrow.

The progressive

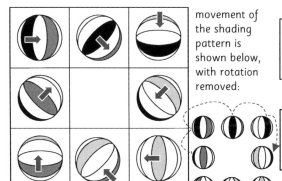

movement of the shading pattern is shown below, with rotation removed:

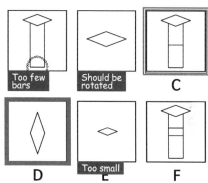

A  B  C

D  E  F

## Answers 17, 18

The number of elements in the left cell is the number of horizontal lines in the right cell.

The element in the middle cell is rotated 90° and

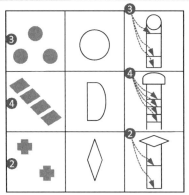

shrunk to sit at the top of the other parts of the right cell.

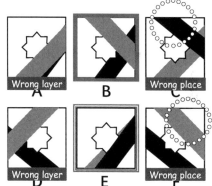

Too few bars    Should be rotated    C

D    Too small    F

## Answers 19, 20

Within each row, the black element is in a constant position, but the grey element rotates clockwise around the cell.

Between each cell and the cell to the

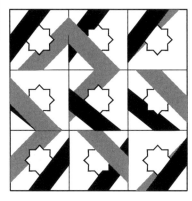

right or below, the black element and the grey element exchange places, behind versus in front of the central star.

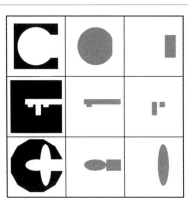

Wrong layer    B    Wrong place

Wrong layer    E    Wrong place

## Answers 21, 22

In each row, the shapes in the middle and right cells are combined and "deleted" or "cut out" from a large black shape on the left.

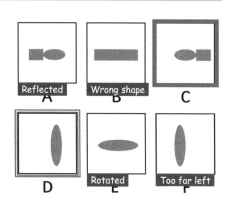

Reflected    Wrong shape    C

D    Rotated    Too far left

Go to the next page

Answers

In each row, the central cell is made of the element in the left cell with the element in the right cell superimposed.

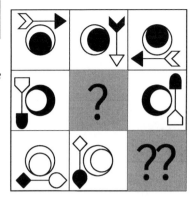

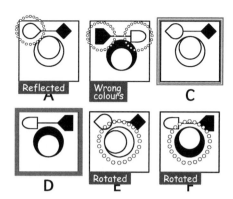

Answers 25, 26

Each row has a shape in common (shown here). In each column there is a shape in common (as shown below). Each cell shows the shapes overlapping, with neither obscuring the other.

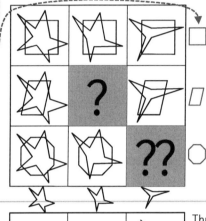

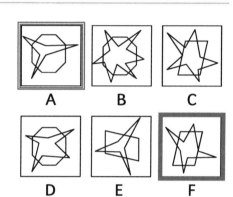

Answers 27, 28

Each cell has a circle. In each column there is a cell with four lines, and two other cells with the same four lines shared amongst the two cells.

Thus each line is present twice in the column.

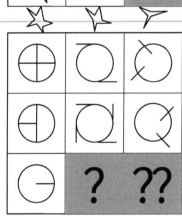

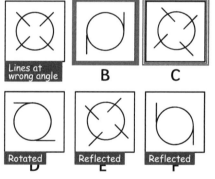

Answers 29, 30

In each row, the central round element rotates anticlockwise.

The outer element rotates clockwise, but with the colours of its end parts swapping between white and black.

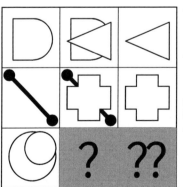

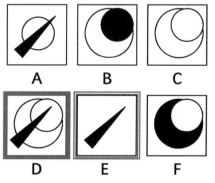

This is the end of this session.

# Training Session 10

Congratulations, non-verbal ninja! You are at the final training session for matrices. You are at the top level of advanced ninja skill with matrix questions.

In this final session consolidate all that you have learnt and aim for the highest possible score.

Questions  1, 2

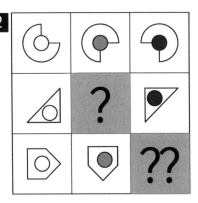

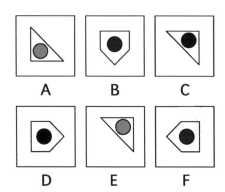

Questions 3, 4

8

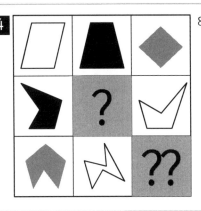

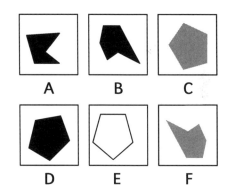

Questions 5, 6

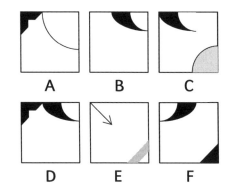

Go to the next page

Questions **7, 8**

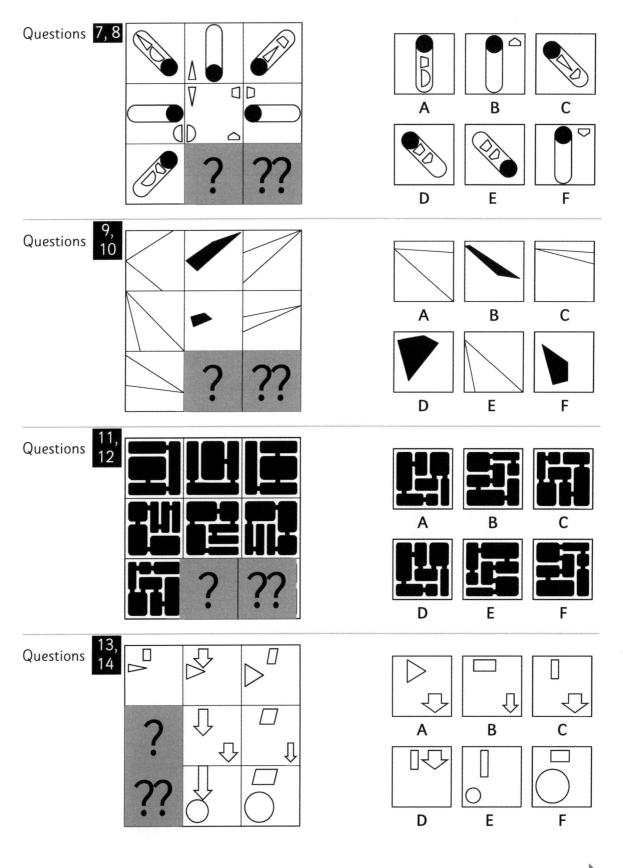

Questions **9, 10**

Questions **11, 12**

Questions **13, 14**

Go to the next page ➡

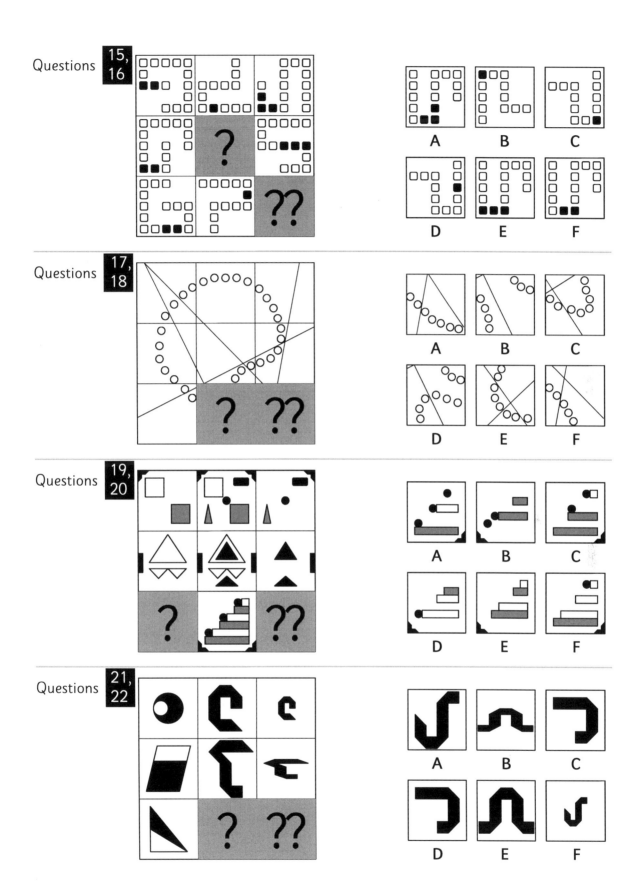

Questions 15, 16

Questions 17, 18

Questions 19, 20

Questions 21, 22

Go to the next page

Questions 23, 24

Questions 25, 26

Questions 27, 28

Questions 29, 30

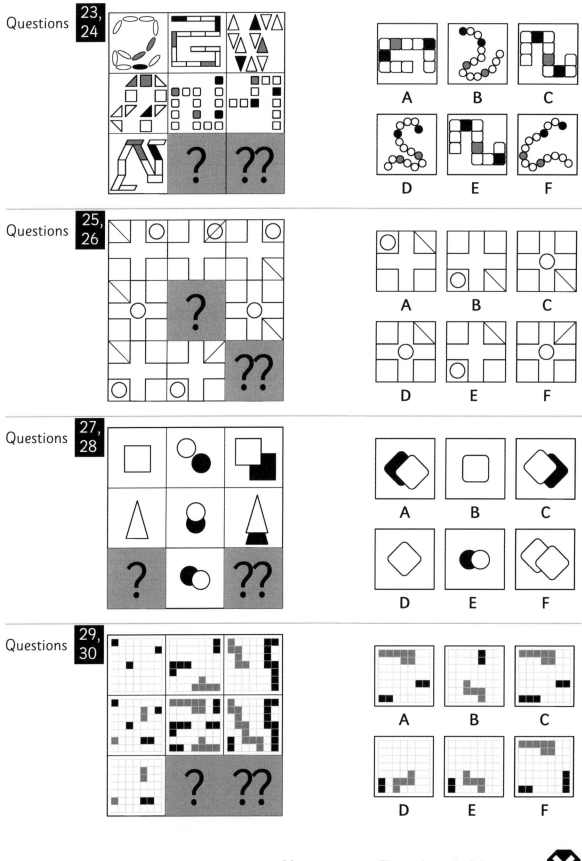

A    B    C

D    E    F

80        This is the end of this session.

Once you have completed all parts of the *Non-Verbal Ninja Training Course*, try out the experience of tackling these questions in the environment of a full range of exam questions, for example in the *11+ Confidence* Practice Exam Papers.

## Answers 1, 2

Each row has one outer element, in three orientations. It rotates clockwise 90°.

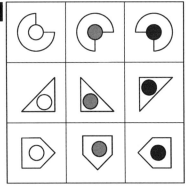

There is also an inner element, which is a disc coloured white, grey, and black in the three respective columns.

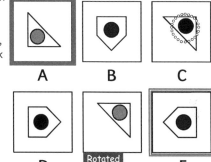

## Answers 3, 4

The shape is a polygon with a certain number of sides and a certain colour.

The numbers of sides vary with the row, from 4 to 6.

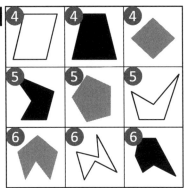

The colours are arranged so that each row (and each column) has one white, one grey and one black element.

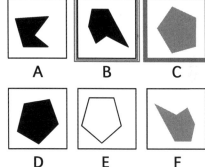

## Answers 5, 6

At the four places where four cells join, there are shapes with double mirror symmetry, lying with one quarter in each cell. The outer corners of the matrix may be part of a similar pattern extending

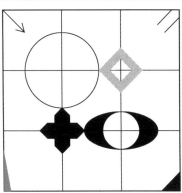

over a larger area (but deciding on this is not necessary to answer the question).

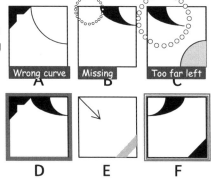

Go to the next page

## Answers  7, 8

There is an array of 8 cylinders arranged around the outer 8 cells, at 45° turns.

Each mid-side cell (top, bottom, left, right) has an element which has a reflected image in the central cell.

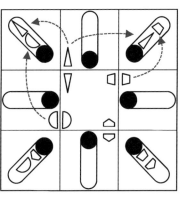

The cylinders in the corner cells have a copy of the small element from each adjacent side cell (two of these relationships are highlighted with arrows).

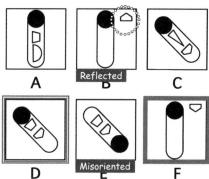

## Answers  9, 10

The lines in the left column and the lines in the right column, when combined, define a quadrilateral by their overlap zone, which is shaded in black in the middle column.

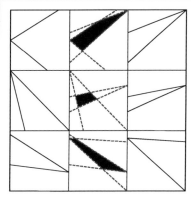

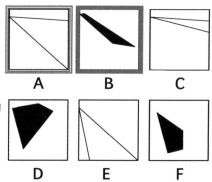

## Answers  11, 12

In each row the design rotates clockwise along the row.

At the same time, one of the connectors between the black regions moves one step clockwise into the gap

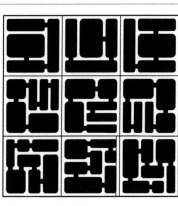

or, equivalently, the gap moves one step anticlockwise.

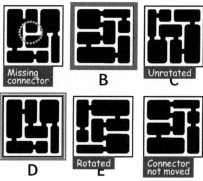

## Answers 13, 14

Once you solve the 1st unknown cell (based on the wide arrow), you learn the direction in which the rectangle is being extended and can then solve the 2nd unknown cell.

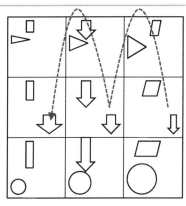

Each row contains an element that is progressively stretched in one or both dimensions. The same occurs for the element in each column.

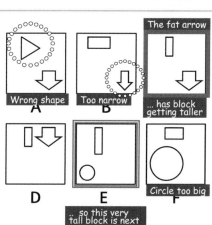

Go to the next page

## Answers 15, 16

In each column the design rotates anticlockwise. The shading pattern moves along the chain of elements, by the number of elements that are shaded. That is to say, by 2 elements in the left column,

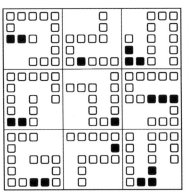

1 element in the middle column and 3 elements in the right column.

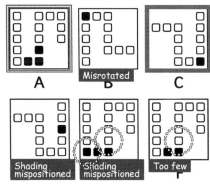

A

B — Misrotated

C

D — Shading mispositioned

E — Shading mispositioned

F — Too few

## Answers 17, 18

There is a continuous chain of circles, and four straight lines, in the overall matrix of 3 x 3 cells, crossing the boundaries of individual cells.

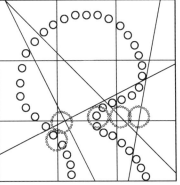

To select the correct answer, look closely at the adjacent cells and look for options that would be a suitable continuation of what you can already see.

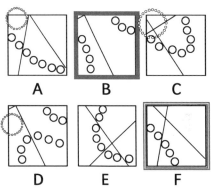

A

B

C

D

E

F

## Answers 19, 20

The left and right columns combined make the central column.

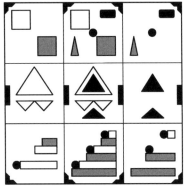

A would pair with E, but E has the lower bar colours in the wrong order.

Similarly, B would pair with F, but B has a misplaced black disc.

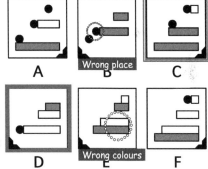

A

B — Wrong place

C

D

E — Wrong colours

F

## Answers 21, 22

In the left cell, there is a pair of elements, a black one in the background and a white one in the foreground. The white element is reduced, either in one dimension or in both, by a certain amount. This reduction is

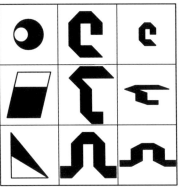

applied to the shape in the middle cell to make the shape in the right cell.

In the bottom row, the triangle is halved in height, so find a pair of shapes differing in height only by two-fold.

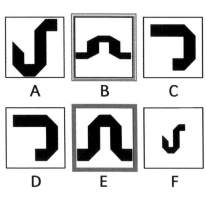

A

B

C

D

E

F

Go to the next page ➡

Answers

Each cell contains a chain of elements. Within each column, the chains all have the same number of elements and are shaded in the same sequence.

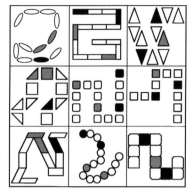

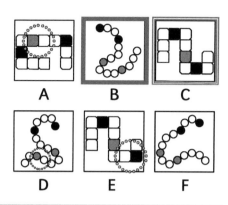

Answers

Each row has a circle in a particular, identical, position in each cell.

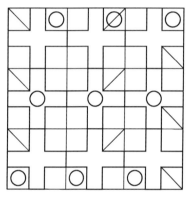

Each column has a diagonal line in a particular, identical position in each cell.

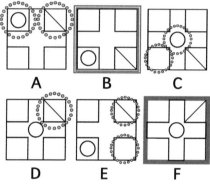

Answers

The element in the left cell appears twice in the right cell. The two copies are displaced from each other slightly, by a distance and in a direction indicated by the

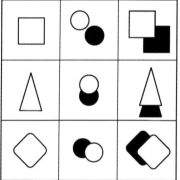

two discs in the central cell.

One of the copies is shaded black and is at the back layer.

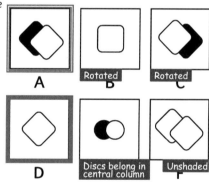

Answers

In each column, the middle cell is composed of an overlap of the upper and lower cells.

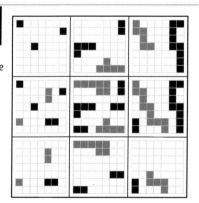

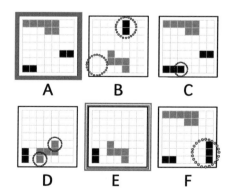

84          This is the end of this session.

Printed in Great Britain
by Amazon